Intimate Devotions For The Insanely Busy

5 Minutes With God Is Not an Impossibility...

David K. Schum

Copyright 2015 by David K. Schum

All rights reserved. No portion of this book may be reproduced, stored in a retrieval system, or transmitted in any form or by any means—electronic, mechanical, photocopy, recording, scanning, or other—except for brief quotations in critical reviews or articles, without the prior written permission of the author.

Scripture taken from *The Message*. Copyright © 1993, 1994, 1995, 1996, 2000, 2001, 2002. Used by permission of NavPress Group.

Scripture quotations noted *NASB* are from THE NEW AMERICAN STANDARD BIBLE. Copyright © The Lockman Foundation, 1960, 1962, 1963, 1968, 1971, 1972, 1973, 1975, 1977, 1995. Used by permission. (www.Lockman.org)

Scripture quotations noted *AMP* are from THE AMPLIFIDE BIBLE. Copyright The Lockman Foundation 1954, 1958, 1962, 1964, 1965, 1987 by the Lockman Foundation. Used by permission. (www.Lockman.org)

Scripture quotations noted KJV are from the King James Version.

Acknowledgements

Thank you Papa, Jesus, and You Holy Spirit, for Your encouragement and love.

Thank you: Adrian, Avery, Cathy, Cheri, Dennis, Duane, George, Heath, Hunter, Jennifer, Jenny, Jim, Jolena, Judy, Laura, Linda, Peyton, Steve, and Stan. Blessings to you all!

Introduction

Everyone needs a Father. It doesn't matter what your religion is or lack of religion is, you need a Father. I don't care what your Christian denomination is, you need a Father. Whether atheist, agnostic or anarchist, everyone needs a final authority figure to talk things over.

This book is a collection of my interactions with my Heavenly Father. It's His relationship with me explained through my quirky, "David filter" if you will. My hope and prayer is you'll recognize a dialogue between He and I that will make you comfortable talking with a loving, personal God. I hope you'll say, "I've had those thoughts before." Or "Can I talk with God like this, it seems so casual?" I believe God is wholly devoted to us, humankind, not just in the universal sense but in the very "mostest" mundane areas of our lives. No matter where you spend your devotional time, your cubicle, airplane seat, car, laundry room, dorm room, shower, and even the toilet, ALL these can be devotional or prayer times, scattered throughout our day. Don't be discouraged, thinking, "I don't have the time, I'm insanely busy!" Just take your devotion time and prayer time in smaller portions. The Bible says, it's the small foxes that spoil the vine. Well, let's set a trap for them, and get them out of our lives.

I would like to take God out of a box if He's been placed there. Some pages contain dialogues, most are headlined, but they are different to view God hopefully, more intimately.

You're loved, prayed for, paid for and have extravagant favor!!!

Jesus, the Billionaire Hotdog Vendor...

I think sometimes I, maybe we, look at Jesus as the King of Kings and the Lord of Lords as we would a wealthy owner of a restaurant chain. We go to the fancy restaurant hoping that the owner might show up so we could get a glimpse of Him. Maybe He will even walk past our table and ask how our food and service was, hoping, just hoping, that there may be some sort of interaction. He is so difficult to see, because He is soooooo busy with all His other work.

What we don't realize is we've walked passed Him a thousand times, not recognizing Him outside of where WE want Him. He is on the street with the everyday man, woman or child passing Him by, or stopping and eating at His hot dog stand. He is out there in front of everybody, serving up the best food to all who come to Him. No cost, it's on the House. Plain dogs, red hots, mustard, sauerkraut, peppers, or chili cheese. He's not scared of His food, and not scared of you dropping chili down the front of your suit. He doesn't even break the flow of work. He just hands you a wad of napkins with a big grin. As you wipe off chili, the stain just disappears, as if it had never happened.

Jesus is accessible, anytime, anywhere, ready

with something to eat or drink, and a wad of napkins. Whether you stay and talk, or take it to go, He's there. If we wait around, he'll even eat one with us, and talk with us, with His mouth full, because He has so much to say, and we have so little time.

It's your choice of what you order, plain or all the way. Your choice of how far you go. Just ask for all of it. It's sometimes messy. Napkins galore . . . yes, but eat there continuously, and you'll get the hang of it. He loves you very much, and wants you to enjoy all of Him. Ask Him, don't be shy. Live life on the edge and ask Him to fix you up, whatever He wants. He might slip a pepper in there, and our eyes may water and our mouth may feel like cloven tongues of fire. I've had my eyes water lots times.

Uh, you might wanna check your mouth there. Yeah, it's mustard . . . nope, nope, the other side. That's it, got it.

Ya Big Brute ...

Sent this to someone who was having a great difficulty in their life yesterday. Thought y'all might enjoy it.

Starting in Matthew 8:24, the key to a stormy situation is maintaining peace. Jesus was so peaceful about his Father taking care of Him and the disciples that he fell asleep in a boat when it started going through a storm. He kept sleeping until they awakened them. He rebuked the storm, and then the disciples for a lack of faith. They had the power all along to rebuke the storm, but were waiting on God to do something. They were mad at Jesus for laying down on the job. But He was doing His job of teaching the disciples who they really were in Him, and exposed a weakness in them, as well.

However, the storm wasn't meant to expose their weakness, but was meant to expose their strength in Him. We have such a failure mentality sometimes. Tests are there to expose what you have learned from God, and how to apply that information on the spur of the moment to bring the Prince of Peace into a situation with what you have already learned. The tests are not supposed to be flipped around and used to blame the Teacher. Focus on what can happen, and not on what you can't do, or what He supposedly hasn't done.

Instead of crying out in panic, "Master, don't You care we are perishing?!" they could have nudged him, and in a peaceful voice asked, "Hey, Master, didn't want to disturb you, but we're sinking. Any ideas what we can do?"

"Yes, rebuke it."

Same result would have happened, except they would've been astonished that the waves and the wind actually obeyed them in Him. Imagine that boat if the disciples could have done that. Nothing would have been heard but the water lapping on the sides of the boat.

Then the Sons of Thunder would have erupted with, "Jesus, Jesus, Jesus!!!!!"

And Jesus would be all, "I told you the same and greater. I told you, I told you, I told you, I'm just sayin'."

You are a brute in your faith. Ask Him how to rebuke whatever storm. It may look like He's lying down, but He's listening to every word even if His back is to you. Listen if His back is to you. That's not abandonment. That means He trusts you more, and maybe you don't need an encouraging look from Him to do something. He'll tell you. I dare you to maybe even take a nap before you ask. Get peaceful. Then ask.

Matthew 6:33 ...

Seek first the Kingdom, and His righteousness and all these things will be added to you. This of course was preceded by a discourse on what the people around Him were worried about.

What are you worried about, what is it you feel like you're being short changed on?
Seek first the Kingdom and His righteousness. I often wondered why He said, "... and His righteousness." I kinda thought the two went hand and hand. BUT, I have met people that were righteousness minded but not Kingdom minded. Kinda legalistic. I have also met people who were all about the Kingdom, but had little righteousness, because it ended up they wanted to build their kingdom instead. The conclusion? You can't build His Kingdom on your righteousness. And you can't build your kingdom on His righteousness. When I meditate on this more and more, I realize this is another grace lifestyle idea ... His Kingdom, His righteousness.
My joy (I almost said job) is to seek first how this can be manifested in my life, and then allow His Kingdom and righteousness to flow through me.

Mud Daubers...

I have a friend Clinton Page Parks, who was having a hard time with life and direction, just trying to figure out God. He was sitting on a bank beside what could've been a creek, pond, tank, or a lake. As he was pondering, He noticed a mud dauber rolling mud to take back, applying the black Fresco on another wall of its nest.

He just felt The Lord speak to him and say, "If I can place purpose in an insect with a tiny, tiny brain, don't you think I have plan and purpose for your life?" An incredible epiphany!

Now, Clint is going to read this and I asked him to editorialize it since it's his story. But my point in telling this is, there are eleventy billion creatures on this planet that have a purpose ecologically, and a purpose that's spiritual — to keep us pointed to the Father.

This is Clint Park's encounter. If you're having trouble with the inner witness at times; look outside at what He's created for us, to best witness Him.

Romans 1:19-20 AMP

For that which is known about God is evident to them and made plain in their inner consciousness, because God [Himself] has shown it to them. For ever since the creation of the world His invisible nature and attributes, that is, His eternal power and divinity, have been made intelligible and clearly discernible in and through the things that have been made (His handiworks). So [men] are without excuse [altogether without any defense or justification],

Gentile Prayers ...

"And when you are praying, do not use meaningless repetition as the Gentiles do, for they suppose that they will be heard for their many words. So do not be like them; for your Father knows what you need before you ask Him. (Matthew 6:7-8 NASB)

I had the Lord repeat one of my prayers back to me, and then He reminded me of this verse above. I was pretty gentile sounding, even for a born-again gentile. You know, you just can't hide a red face from the Lord. I realized if I used one of my friend's names in a conversation as much as I used "Father," they would think me a bit daft.

"Hi. James. How are you, James?"

"How's your day, James?"

"How's the wife, James, the kids, James, your business, James?"

His thoughts would be "What does this guy want from me?" Selah ...

Now really, what do you want from God? A relationship, or stuff?

Then Jesus says, "Pray this way, 'Father' ..." He

addresses Him by name once, then uses personal pronouns the rest of the time. Get that . . . PERSONAL pronouns. He builds a personal conversation with God.

It peeled the selfishness and manipulation out of my prayer life. And made me very mindful of my vain repetitions in prayer, and exploded my intimacy with Him. I now think about my relationship with Him before I pray. As one of my favorite speakers, Graham Cooke says, "I craft a prayer."

Salt and Ketchup on Request...

Bless the Lord, O my soul, And all that is within me, bless His holy name. Bless the Lord, O my soul, And forget none of His benefits; (Psalms 103:1-2 NASB)

"Papa, show me all Your benefits..."

"You first, David. You show me all that is within you, and I'll show you all that is within Me. I know that sounds pretty contractual to you. But it's really an exchange of what's inside of each other. You see, what I have to exchange is backed up by My Son, My Spirit, the Word, My throne, all of Heaven, the universe, and the earth you live on. And I gave it all to you packaged in Jesus. What do you have?"

"Me and my choice to bless You."

"Perfect, I'll take it... You want that to go?"

"I'll dine in. Thanks."

"Order up... I need a Jesus all the way. Time the courses though, I think he'll be here a while — finally."

Simple

"David, you want what I have?"

"Yes, Sir . . ."

"Live in My moment, not yours . . ."

It's Not a Village ... People.

Today's is a bit edgy, may not be for everyone. Just sayin'.

To say that it takes a village to raise a child, is like saying it takes a tower to get to God. We do the work in the flesh to try and get to God or raise a child, and pat ourselves on the back for our accomplishments. But in the end, we all are confused and sound like "Babel-ing idiots." (Psycho-babel advice is given on how to raise and protect your children.) We work so hard to get to Him, when all along God is willing to come down to us, to raise us to raise children. (He humbles Himself yet again.) We need to be His trusting children, to raise trusting children.

I need to focus on the vertical relationship with God, not in tower building, but trusting Him to impact my horizontal relationships of my village, and possibly your kids.

Crazy Track Meet

Imagine a track meet with a race of hurdlers, where the gun fires and they sprint towards the first hurdles. When they get there, they stop, carefully climb over them, give themselves high fives, and then start toward the next hurdle, only to stop and do the same thing over and over. They never use the momentum of the first hurdle to carry them to the next and to the next, so on and so on.

I think I do God that way at times. I look at His accomplishment as mine, talk about it, study it, high five myself, all the while He's telling me, "Keep going!" But I'm losing the momentum. To finish the race under His coaching requires me not to focus on the hurdle, but the race's finish.

I'm going to focus on the finish and hurdle the hurdles, by maintaining the momentum . . .
We move from glory to glory!
2 Corinthians 3:18

Big Father is Watching...

He is Omnipresent, He is always around, wherever you are He is there, whatever you're doing He is there. He is not the Gestapo; He is not the KGB, CIA, or the NSA. He is not ever present to spy on you and call you out on every infraction. He is a Father that is there to help. He has been to every ballgame, school play, band concert, college frat party, business meeting, presentation, car accident, and even on death's door. He is there always!

GOD, investigate my life; get all the facts firsthand. I'm an open book to You; even from a distance, You know what I'm thinking. You know when I leave and when I get back; I'm never out of your sight. You know everything I'm going to say before I start the first sentence. I look behind me and You're there, then up ahead, and You're there, too — Your reassuring presence, coming and going. This is too much, too wonderful — I can't take it all in!

Is there any place I can go to avoid your Spirit, to be out of your sight? If I climb to the sky, You're there! If I go underground, You're there! If I flew on morning's wings to the far western horizon, You'd find me in a minute — You're already there waiting! Then I said to myself, "Oh, He even sees me in the dark! At night I'm immersed in the light!" It's a fact: darkness isn't dark to You; night and day, darkness and light, they're all the same to You."

Investigate my life, O God, find out everything about me. Cross-examine and test me, get a clear picture of what I'm about. See for yourself whether I've done anything wrong — then guide me on the road to eternal life. (Psalm 139:1-12, 23-24 MSG)

Several years ago, I received news that some friends of ours had just lost their son in a tragic car accident. I was very, very upset. I started packing to go to Austin to . . . well, do what Jesus did best and stop a funeral. I was bound and determined to raise their son back from the dead. While I was packing, the Lord stopped me, and told me not to pack, but unpack and stay home. Well, I was distraught. I knew I had the faith to do what Jesus did. So the Lord showed me a quick glimpse of this young man in heaven. It was almost like a summer camp atmosphere. Then the Lord spoke to me and said, "'His name' is settled in and we haven't stopped laughing since he's been here." That was it — so simple and so settling.

Our complex emotions in a tragic situation like that are enormous. The Lord never said he was too young, it was a tragic accident. The Lord was focused on their laughter in heaven: a sense of humor, and non-stop laughter. It was heaven's perspective about the present moment in heaven and not on an insurmountable loss on earth.

You know… Ephesians 3:20-21 is like . . .
Ah — what the Hee Haw — the Amplified Bible says it all . . .

Now to Him Who, by (in consequence of) the [action of His] power that is at work within us, is able to [carry out His purpose and] do superabundantly, far over and above all that we [dare] ask or think [infinitely beyond our highest prayers, desires, thoughts, hopes, or dreams]-- To Him be glory in the church and in Christ Jesus throughout all generations forever and ever. Amen (so be it).

You Are Your Own Stimulus Package ...

In Jeremiah God commands the captives to seek the welfare of the city. Not a welfare check, or housing allowance, or food stamps. Actually go in and be the blessing for the city. You are the stimulus package; YOU are the welfare check to the city. You carry the blessing of God inside you to be a blessing.

Spend your money in the city. Instead of always changing your own oil, let someone else do it on occasion. And when you're in there, bless that business, pray for witty ideas and inventions, find out if and where the workers go to church, etc.

And church people, TIP the wait people. If you want them to read a tract, PAY them to do it. On Sundays and Wednesdays there should be a positive cash flux in the hands of wait people. The church crowd should be a blessing, not a curse. Remember, with the same measure you tip, God will tip you. Ask the Lord how you can bless our economy locally. Be the blessing God intends you to be.

And seek (inquire for, require, and request) the peace and welfare of the city to which I have caused you to be carried away captive; and pray to the Lord for it,

for in the welfare of [the city in which you live] you will have welfare. (Jeremiah 29:7 AMP)

Just a Trim ...

"Lord, I almost lost it yesterday. Just need a trim."

"Okay."

"Hey ... Those are loppers."

"Yeah, they're good for cutting off big, dead branches. Slice. And here ... slice."

"Wait ... oh, wow! That one, too? Hey, I'm practically naked here!"

"David, I can cover you, or there are some fig leaves over there. Your choice."

"You, I want You to cover me."

"Good answer! David, My definition of much fruit is different from yours. Here, the Holy Spirit wants to paint Himself over the pruned areas. You don't want anything to grow back where things just got pruned. Much fruit, David."

Gods in Control, but Who'd He Leave in Charge?

Me thinks us, we, within the church, are a bit double-minded, bi-polar, and unstable in our ways.

When it comes to salvation, we, for the most part, are Arminianists. It is our choice to accept and walk in what we've been chosen for (salvation). When it comes to the gifts of the Holy Spirit, we become Calvinistic. If God wants me to have them, He'll slap them on me. Sorry, that was a bit rough, but only for brevity sake.

How come if grace is so irresistible, that we can't resist it to get us out of sin and saved, but somehow it loses its power after we get saved, and we step back into sin?

Why do we use God's love on people to get them in the Kingdom, but use fear of God tactics afterwards to keep them in line?

And why do people tell me God's teaching them a lesson through their back pain, and yet they're in my office to get out of back pain. If God is teaching them a lesson through back pain, why prolong the lesson by coming to my office? Does that make me, a Doctor, a devil's advocate?

And on the lighter side . . .

Graham Cooke says, "If Jesus is making intercession for you, find out what He's praying, and come into agreement with that."

Bill Johnson another favorite author, says, "God can't give you what He doesn't have."

I'm not Spock...

"David, it's not controlling your emotions that pleases Me. You're not a Vulcan. It's your believing Me and your obedience to Me, no matter which way your emotions are headed. That's faith..."

Owwwww!!!

Dang it! I scraped my knee when I fell. I hope no one saw. How humiliating.

Pride comes before a fall.

Ever notice that when we are humiliated it's because of a pride issue. But if we are humbled, it's a teachable heart issue. "Lord, keep us humble, keep us teachable."

Controlling Control...

'Whatcha doing, David?"

"Trying to get a handle on this one area in life and it's flopping around like a fish."

"Oh, look. The fish has a name on it. What's it read?"

"Control."

"Ahhhh, so you're trying to control control? How's that working for ya?"

"Slimy, jumpy, and getting stuck with fins."

"So really, control has a hold on you, not you on it?"

"Yes, apparently."

"Well, why don't you let flopping fish lie? Come over here with Me, sit next to Me. My presence has a tendency to dry up the sliminess."

Jesus Jumped on Top of That Sin Grenade ...

Love covers is an interesting concept, and one I always attributed to God. But in 1 Peter 4 it's our command, along with being fervent in our love towards one another. Love helps us put the pin back in the grenade for the sake of others.

Love covers a multitude of sin. Do we deny sin exists? I don't think so. Do we turn a blind eye and let it continue? No, I believe not. We handle it like Jesus in John 8, with the woman caught in adultery. We handle it like the Holy Spirit handles the sin in our life, covering it in so much love that He chokes the death out of sin, to bring life to us through repentance in Christ.

A hardened heart is the one that loves to expose people for who they "really" are. As Danny Silk puts it, "There are those who love to tell the truth, and those who tell the truth in love."

"Lord, cover, cover, cover us, as you love, love, love us, and we each other."

Void ...

"Lord, what's this void inside this morning?"

"That void is from a-void-ance. You a-void doing something I want you to do so that creates a vacuum of disobedience. If you love me you'll obey me. What you're missing, that void, is the love that comes with obeying me."

10 minutes later after obeying Him . . .

"Lord, what's that You're doing?"

"I'm singing . . ."

"Why are you singing?"

"I'm singing over you because you obeyed Me. And that need, the one bigger than you — I'm meeting it."

"For just obeying You in that little thing?"

"David, obedience is never little to Me. It's saturated in love, your love towards Me.

Jesus, the Perfect Armor Bearer...

My pastor Stan Roberts taught a great lesson yesterday on Ephesians 6 and the Armor of God. He went through the individual pieces and explained them, the Roman use and our spiritual use. Thanks again, Pastor Stan! It reminded me how Jesus gave up His armor that we might gain it .

He gave up the helmet of salvation and took on a crown of thorns. He dropped His shield of faith for us so that one hand might be nailed to a tree. He dropped the sword of the Spirit, and the other hand was nailed. His robe, like the belt of truth, stolen, gambled away. The breast plate of righteousness was removed; He was stabbed with a spear. His shod feet of the Gospel, bare, was nailed to the cross. And He never ceased praying for the ones condemning Him, as we need to.

He became naked, so we wouldn't fight naked. He was the perfect Armor Bearer. He willingly gave up His Armor, so that we could stand as He did, live as He did, and fight like He did. As Pastor Stan said, "His Armor will always fit us perfectly."

And the only reason you put your armor on every morning is because you take it off at night? Selah.

Favor...

The favor of God on our life started with the death and burial, and then exploded with the resurrection of Jesus Christ. We have had almost 2000 years of God's favor snowballing towards us when we got saved, and it continues to grow.

Quit trying to control it and just enjoy the ride!

"Obey" — the Harsh Four-Letter Word...

Obedience is not what you think it is, but what He thinks it is.

It's Not Just RAAAAAAHHHH!

Clarity of thought isn't necessarily coming from a lack of busyness, chaos or distractions. It comes from us choosing Jesus to be Jesus, no matter what mountain is before us, or what beautiful, peaceful mountain glade is created in its place once the mountain is removed.

If we are so goal oriented that all we care about is moving mountains, and not looking at what Jesus wants to do with us afterwards, then we are simply a mountain-moving company of faith.

Working on the mountain glade afterwards is what makes us more than conquerors. Bringing order to chaos is one thing, maintaining order and increasing the end result is another. That's going from glory to glory.

It's not just RAAAAAAHHHH!

It's the peaceful humming afterwards.

Lessons from Norman

When I was attending Parker College of Chiropractic in Dallas, Texas, I had gross anatomy. We named our cadaver Norman. I won't go into the details except this; sometimes there was a structure that was hidden under other structures. Like a nerve hidden under some layers of muscle that we would have to expose because we were going to be tested on it. You could look at the dissection manual, anatomy atlases, even ask the instructor. But really, it was a hands-on approach that they were after. Not a hack job, but a finely, teased out process to find the nerve that you needed.

Getting into God's word is like that. You can ask others and look up stuff in commentaries, but really, it's between you and your ability to meditate on God's word, using the Holy Spirit to guide you into what you are going to be tested on next. And, dissecting and teasing out every bit of testable information.

With God, it's always an open book test, but it's best to find out ahead of time what your test material is going to be. The Great Instructor wants you to learn, but there's not a lot of talking during tests. That's what class is for.

Progressive Thinking . . .

"Papa, sometimes I feel as if You have disappointed me in the past."

"I can see why you would feel that way. But why is it I'm not disappointed in you and your past?"

"Well, Jesus absolutely dealt with my past."

"And He hasn't dealt with Mine?"

"Uh, oh . . . What do you mean?"

"The reason you have felt disappointed with Me in some areas, is because you didn't let Jesus absolutely deal with your future in those areas. You felt your future was your responsibility. My Son is the same yesterday, today, and forever. He handles everything, past, present, and future. We are not just about absolutely dealing with your sin, but everything in your life. You simply stopped believing Us to handle your future. Do you remember what you told your patient yesterday? 'There is a process to progress.' You stopped the process, because you stopped looking at the future through Our eyes and looked at the surroundings, not Who surrounds you. You can blame Me if you want, I can take it. But it will slow your progress.

David, hope does not disappoint."

"I'm good, thank you. I lost the blame game . . . again." :-)

He Hears You ...

We often strive to hear His voice. Everyone wants to be loved on, nurtured, wisdom evoked, as we need it. But do you think He strives to hear us? I think He did, and does. He strove through Jesus. No one can ever really say, "God, You're up there and we're down here, you don't understand." Jesus erases that argument. He was tempted in every way, and yet never sinned.

Listen, I know God knows everything. But with Jesus' life here on earth — God on earth as a man, He hears you. He hears you through the entire life of Jesus; recorded and un-recorded events, death, burial, resurrection, and ascension. He sits at the right hand of the Father, and intercedes for you. Because of Jesus, God really does know what it's like to be us.

He hears you — loud, screaming, crying, quiet, brooding, ecstatic, angry, frustrated, hopeless, laughing, and fearful — He hears you. And He is working on your behalf.

Dripping Faucet...

"Papa, why do you constantly tell me to trust You."

"Because, I am like a dripping faucet. You don't pay attention to it until everything is quiet, and you're trying to sleep. You can tighten me down; you can call someone to fix it for you. But I'm not after that kind of experience for you. I want a hands on experience, you and I working together to find the trust leak."
(Silence on my part.)

"Oh, look. There is a small particle of fear that's keeping that from sealing properly. Why don't you pull it out."

"Okay, I see it. It was actually a smaller problem than I realized."

"Yeah, the enemy likes to magnify things so they look bigger than they really are. Better?"

"Wow! Yes. Thank you."
"Sleep well, My friend."

"Love You, thank You."

"Deep breath, and rest in Me."

Flat-lined...

"Papa, running a bit flat-lined in my emotions. Hear the tone?"

"Well, now, I could start with chest compressions, fire up the cardiac paddles. I can get a big shot of adrenaline ready. End result? Broken ribs, burn marks, and a hole in your heart, but you would survive."

"Sounds painful."

"Let me inside your heart, I'll massage it. Now turn over your trust in Me. Your trust in Me, is like a pace maker, as you trust more deeply, you won't need a pace maker. Now I can tell you to trust more, but that sounds so American, as if you're lacking something. But I tell you to trust Me more deeply. Listen, I could cover your heart with layer after layer of trust tape, but it would still be surface. I don't want a surface relationship with you. I want a deep one, built on trust that soaks in deeper and deeper with every beat of your heart."

"Wow, that's kinda heavy for a Monday morning, Lord!"

"Well, you're worth it. I love you."

I'm So Unworthy... Whatever...

Graham Cooke asks, "What is it that you need God to be to you, that He has never been before?"

Some people might see that as a question for God to perform for them. It's not. Either God is everything to you, or He isn't. It's not that God wants to perform, it's He wants to reveal to you a deeper nature of who He can really be in your life. He can plan out your vacation, soccer mom chauffeur schedule, wedding lay out design, etc. God wants to reveal Himself to you in a way that you get to perform, so that you can be as Graham puts it, "A visual aid for the Kingdom." Ask Him, what does He need to be for you today? You can't bug Him enough. Matthew 7:7
A sk
S eek
K nock

"Papa, where are you? Are you upset? You feel kinda distant."

"Over here, not far."

"What're doing?"

"Watching you work. I like watching My children doing what they're designed to do. It's okay, the Spirit is there, He's helping. You know, proud dads stand on the side lines at football practice ... same principle."

"Oh, okay."

"Jesus and I were just talking about some plans for you. He's holding His sides laughing."

"Wait. Is that like football initiation kind of laughing or different?"

"Different. Your eyes have not seen or your ears heard of the things we have planned for you — future and hope kind of things."

"Whew! Okay. Thanks. Just want to make You happy."

"Done."

Will the Real Us Please Stand Up...

If I am to be known in heaven as I am here, how will I be known?

Will I be known as the guy who's always trying to play dead, dying to self? Or the guy that's alive in Christ? If Jesus was 100% God and 100% Man, can't I be 100% Jesus and 100% David? Or, 100% Jesus and 100% James, or Connie, or Doug, or Dennis, Jenny, Bobbie, Jerry, Nina, or Kay—fully integrated into us as we are in Him. As many times as I have tried to "kill" myself, I ought to have a suicide hotline number tattooed on my wrist. It's not about being dead; it's about being alive in Christ. Let's live 100% for Him, in Him, and let Him bring out the best in us to live completely saturated in Him, because of His fully lived life here on earth.

Deep Calls to Deep ...

With the frequency we pray, we can marvel at the frequency of our deepening relationship with the Lord. To pray without ceasing is to deepen our relationship without ceasing.

Psalm 42:7
Deep calls to deep at the sound of Your waterfalls; All Your breakers and Your waves have rolled over me.
(Psalm 42:7 NASB)

Joys of Summer...

When I was a kid, the big thing for a yard was to get a load of sandy loam and spread it on top of the grass to raise the level of the yard. I didn't care about that though. It was the big pile of cool, cool dirt that begged to be excavated with Tonka® trucks, digging, pushing, with lots of construction noises and spit. None of this fancy beep, beep, beep, as trucks backed up, and your hand just got run over.

Hot, tired, sweaty, that's when the tunneling started, and we'd dig as far as we could, leave our arms in the dirt, just cooling ourselves. Then "King of the Hill" would start. Whoever won got to collapse the tunnels.

God has a big pile of dirt for you to play in, if you're not too busy playing adult. That pile could be worship, the Word, revelation, knowledge, or just simple fellowship with Him. Get in there, get dirty and sweaty. (Really, when was the last time you sweated in fun with God?) We have to remain childlike, in order to continue to see heaven manifesting in our lives. Dig deep!

God KNOWS your past, and He KNOWS your future. But the only way He can deal with either is in the here and now, the present. Don't disregard the gentle tug of the Holy Spirit to work in you today, so He can deliver you from your past and into your future. Today's the day!

It's His Curriculum, and the Classroom, Your Heart.

Jesus didn't come to live here, die here, and be raised from the dead here to have us merely put human attributes on God so He would agree with us here on earth. The attributes of God dwarf, to the nth degree, our human attributes. BUT yet He still chooses, in His humility, to talk with us in a language that is our own, our native tongue. But the language is even deeper than that. The heart language that God listens to is a universal language. There is no race, creed, or color in the heart language.

How many times have we said, "Well, if I were God, I'd do this and this." Well, there is a reason, thankfully so, that we're not God. Tacking our humanness on God is . . . well, tacky.

He is all knowing, all powerful, and ever present. If we were God in our situation, we would probably place ourselves in the exact same spot, because that is what is best for us — to learn HIS attributes, HIS humility, and HIS love. We learn from Him, we do not instruct Him.

For who has known the mind of the Lord, that he will instruct Him?
But we have the mind of Christ.
(1 Corinthians 2:16 NASB)

Run-on prayers...

There is much to be said for prayer, a never ending dialog between Creator and creation. Sometimes in the dialog nothing is said because the connection says it all. Sometimes there's a lot of listening on His part, and sometimes a lot on my part.

Paul says to pray without ceasing. How? In the busyness of our day, how? Very simply, stay connected. It's like being on a divine speaker phone. How many times have we been on the phone and said, "Hang on," as we put the milk up. We stay connected, and do what needs to be done. And let's don't even mention trying to find the mute button when running for the bathroom because the conversation is so good. :-)
That's like prayer without cessation.

Let's Ask Ourselves These Questions...

What am I in Christ?
Who am I in Christ?
How am I in Christ?
Where am I in Christ?
Why am I in Christ?

If we can't answer these questions definitively, now is not the time to play the man card and not ask for directions. We need to do some soul searching, allowing the Word to be our lamp, and the Spirit to be our guide as He maps out the four W's and H for us. He will. He's faithful.

He knows...

When walking around the Howard Payne University campus one night, I was looking at the old street lamps that lit the campus. I think they were given by the class of, like 1938, or something. Anyway, He started talking to me about the worker that set the lamp post and bolted it down. He knew everything about that man's life, fears, and dreams. The sense of satisfaction he felt when he gave the nut the last bit of torque. Then the one that ran the wire, then the one that made the wire and coated it, the miner that mined the copper ore, the ones who that have changed the light bulbs over the years.

Your phone ... He knows the thoughts in Chinese of the ones that put your smart phone together. He knows the thoughts of 6.5 billion current residents of this earth, past residents, and future residents. No backups, no battery backups, His knowledge is maintained through a deep, deep love for us. The only thing He forgets is our sin. He knows your name, numbers of hairs on your head, everything. You have a question, He has an answer. He's not too busy, you don't have to stand in line, and you don't have to hurry, because someone behind you has a bigger problem. He knows. He loves.

One More Paradox...

Does it rattle you like it does me to come boldly to the throne of grace to receive grace and mercy in a time of need. I mean grovel on your face, or crawl on your knees or on your belly, inching closer to the throne, fearful that His holiness and power would kill you on the spot. We do a piece of stupid forgetfulness, sin or whatever. We might run in and run out, not look Him in the eye, and say thanks over our shoulder. Or we could walk in stiffly; ready to look Him in the eye, ready to take our scolding. Or we could simply walk in, sit at His feet, lean our head on His knee and say, "Papa, I did it again." Or "I shouldn't have . . ." or "I should have . . ."
His hand is on our head and saying "Yeah, I know."

Or we could approach the throne, as a teenager who comes in from (whatever sport) two-a-days practice, hitting the refrigerator with the force of a blocking sled. He realizes it's just been freshly stocked, and walks away with much more than he needs now, but has some for later. He sees his Dad and Brother watching sports, kisses his Dad, and thanks Him for His abundant supply. He winks at his older Brother, thanks Him for stocking the fridge, plops down next to them, and fellowships.

It's a paradox to walk into an ample supply of everything, and have done nothing to earn it.

Whatever, Lord...

Have you ever blown The Lord off like I have?

"David, I love you. You're made in My image. I've created you as the head and not the tail, above only, and not underneath."

"Yeah, yeah. You say that to everyone."

"David, I love it when you sing to Me."

"Thanks. How much do ears plugs cost in heaven? Wait, you probably have a bad voice filter that fixes that."

"David, you sing from your heart, not your mouth. I look at your heart, and listen. I love you."

"Thanks, Lord, but You say that to everyone. "You have to, You're God . . ."

"Well, there's only one David like you, so I can't say it to everyone like you. I don't do cookie cutter, mass production sayings. I craft My words to hit your heart. I talk to you completely, customized to you. You are My custom home. Let Me make My repairs and remodel you. You need more room for Me."

(Repentant silence on my part . . .)

"I love it when You talk to me! Thank you. Is that a crow bar?"

"Growth, David, growth. I need to make a green room in your heart. Someplace where you can cater to Me instead of the other way around."

"Okay, can I close my eyes?"

"Nope watch this." He he he.

Wow, Lord...

"God, I'll never understand You and Your goodness..."

"David, My ways are higher than your ways, and My thoughts than your thoughts. But when you trust Me, My ways become your ways, and My thoughts are yours. Trust Me today, today's the day.

There is Ample Room in the Kingdom for Mistakes.

By practice we hear the voice of The Lord. We practice righteousness.

I practice chiropractic. I can't perfect it, because there are too many variables that walk through the door with every patient. So all I can do is the best I can for who's in front of me with the wisdom and knowledge that God has given me, and pray for the best result.

That's how we practice righteousness in the kingdom. Life would be absolutely boring if we did the exact same thing every time. So we get to deal with imperfect people, some practicing righteousness, some not. We have to deal with the impractical, with the impracticality of faith to get a desired Kingdom result. At times it is completely out of our hands except for trusting Him, and it turns out His way. If not, we don't change our theology, we go to God, and let Him redefine our experience, and hit it again, rather than our experience redefining us and keeping us from growing in Him.

Feeling a Bit Clingy Today?

Hope does not disappoint . . .

Romans 5 is one if the strongest passages in the Word to latch onto and never let go. Hope should be like a piece of cellophane that has static electricity, and no matter how hard you try, you can't get it not to cling to you. Finally, you have someone else pick it off you, but then it clings to them. So, is your hope contagious?

I think we sometimes think that hope is this light weight element that can be so easily brushed off or lost. Not so, quite the opposite. Hope is heavily earned, tribulation, perseverance, proven character, and it doesn't disappoint. It stays in impossible situations. We cling to each other.

Where is that Velcro body suit? I'm feeling a bit clingy today.

Taking the Lord's Name in Vain...

"Whatcha doing?"

"Oh, hey, Lord. Just staying busy."

"Why?"

"Well, You know idle hands, devil's workshop and all."

"Ah, so since when have you canonized an American colloquialism? Huh? You know 'I only help those who help themselves.' That one robs My people of My grace. Help themselves . . . what a joke. Hey, let me test you?"

"Okay."

"Stop what you're doing and come talk to Me."

"Yeah, give me a minute, just about at a stopping place."

"Hey, David, let me test you again."

"Sure . . . wait, what?"

"So busy can't stop, huh? David, unless I build the house, you labor in vain. You're so busy trying to stay out of the devil's workshop; it's made you too busy to enter into My rest. So you do all this work in vain because YOU are trying not to be idle, and then slap My name on it. Thereby you take My name in _____."

"Vain. Ohhhhhhhhh. When can I schedule another retake?"

"Sit down. I'd thought you'd never ask. Next time, let's co-labor together."

Has God Ever Accused You of Doing too Much Good?

The Israelites, while in the desert, took up an offering of the gold they had received from the Egyptians on their way out of the country. They gave and gave and gave, until the Lord told Moses that it is more than enough.

What do we plan on doing today that the Lord would say is more than enough? God gave them the gold in the first place. Then He asked for a free will offering. God gave us His love first, so we can give a free will love offering back. Can we spoil God today?!

Sometimes the Word Says It All!!!

In hope against hope he believed, so that he might become a father of many nations according to that which had been spoken, "So shall your descendants be." Without becoming weak in faith he contemplated his own body, now as good as dead since he was about a hundred years old, and the deadness of Sarah's womb; yet, with respect to the promise of God, he did not waver in unbelief but grew strong in faith, giving glory to God, and being fully assured that what God had promised, He was able also to perform. Therefore it was also credited to him as righteousness.
(Romans 4:18-22 NASB)

The Enemy Has No Originality to Him.

He can only distort the truth. Paint a picture, if you will, over what God's finished painting already is for you. You have a right to tump over the enemy's paints and brushes.

Now to Him who is able to do far more abundantly beyond all that we ask or think, according to the power that works within us, to Him be the glory in the church and in Christ Jesus to all generations forever and ever. Amen. (Ephesians 3:20, 21 NASB)

Where is Our Fear Factor?

Do we fear the Lord so much that we are scared of making a mistake and we do nothing? (Burying a talent.) Or do we love Him so much, and have a desire to please Him, that by not obeying Him brings a fear upon us?

Perfect love casts out fear because fear involves punishment. I believe it's not if we love the Lord we OBEY Him, it's if we LOVE the Lord we obey Him. Love is our motivation to obey Him, not obedience our motivation to love Him.

To fear the Lord is the "beginning" of wisdom, not the end result. Love is the end result.

It's not, where is our fear factor, but where is our love factor?

Hold On...
American Parenting Perspective...

The only way my child can appreciate anything is by them working hard and earning what they get. They'll appreciate it, take care of it and show themselves and others what they can accomplish. They'll take pride in themselves.

The Father's parenting perspective...

Here is my Son. He's a gift. You don't have to work for Him, you have Him. You have free access to Him, as much as you want, as little as you want, or none at all. He loves you. And He even paid the way to access Himself. You can appreciate Him, or not appreciate Him. It doesn't change the fact that God gave Him to you, because He loves you. He took all the work out of it.

If pride's so important in the development of character, why is it just an American virtue and not a Kingdom one?

Tribulation, perseverance, proven character and hope... hope doesn't disappoint. (Romans 5) There's nothing about pride in there. Hope trumps pride.

Hold On 2...
American Parenting Perspective...

I don't want my children to work like I did. I want to provide for them what I couldn't have. Whatever their hearts desire is, I want them to have it. They don't need to suffer like I did and do without. They're entitled to what I couldn't have.

The Father's parenting perspective...

I give you all that I have, to accomplish all I have for you. You'll co-labor with Me, a family business. You're entitled to all I have, because of My Son. You're joint heirs.

Quit trying to convince yourself...

How do you know when you've made progress with the Lord in an area? When you quit convincing yourself you trust the Lord in an area, to you knowing that you know the Lord in an area.

Trusting Him while you are panicked leads to knowing Him in peace and rest. Even if your trust is completely surrounded by fear, trusting the Lord is still trusting The Lord, and He honors that.

Trusting the Lord to do things your way vs. knowing the Lord will do things His way. It'll be so much better than your own.

"Lord, I know You. You're way beyond my concept of Your faithfulness. I won't bring this (whatever) up again unless You do. I know You. Thank You."

Trust and obey leads to knowing His way.

Huh?

"David, when all is going well, there is more. It's not a discontentment on your part that you don't have enough, or a discontentment on My part, that you didn't receive enough. It's more, because I Am more. I Am more than enough. So much so that it will naturally pour out on those around you. It's not an "Us four and no more" mentality — just the three of US and you. It's Us four and everybody else. That's kingdom mindedness. And so it is with everyone else connected to Us through Jesus."

RPPDD

Relay
Pray
Prey
Dismay
Delay

God wants to relay to pray, so you won't become prey to dismay because of a delay.

Cynicism in Scripture...

But he who is spiritual appraises all things, yet he himself is appraised by no one. For who has known the mind of the Lord, that he will instruct Him? But we have the mind of Christ. (1 Corinthians 2:15, 16 NASB)

This is one of the toughest passages in scripture, and yet, the most hopeful. We can sometimes live in a "we against them" mentality. As in, we have a better perspective here on earth in our plights, than they do in heaven. "C'mon God, I'm down here; you're up there." So I think we have a tendency to instruct The Lord how things "really" are, and how He could really help if He did things this way.

But the loss is ours when we try and instruct the Lord. Hence the cynical statement (my opinion) that puts us in our place. The beauty of the promise is that we have the mind of Christ. If Christ Jesus dwells in you, Heaven is seeing things from your prospective. You also have the Heavenly answer in Jesus, readily available to avail through you the answer that you need.

He abides in us, and we in Him, co-laboring together. That relationship can be appraised by no one, because it is invaluable.

Sacrifice of Praise...

When we get hit hard, we may find it hard to praise the Lord. That's why it's a sacrifice: don't feel like it, what's the point, what's the use, couldn't praise our way out of a wet paper bag, yada, yada.

What about when things are awesome. Couldn't be better, everything is going our way, what's the point, everything is great . . . Exactly! That's when we praise Him, when there is no need beyond what we can understand. That's what makes it a sacrifice.

A sacrifice of praise is something we do when we are overwhelmed beyond our comprehension, whether bad or great! Sacrifice in praise until you are exuberant in Him, no matter what the circumstance.

Rewarder...

Hebrews 11 says God is a rewarder of those who diligently seek Him. It is His nature to reward, not hold back. But we are notorious for holding back from Him, just to see "if" He will. What is our due diligence?

Therefore I urge you, brethren, by the mercies of God, to present your bodies a living and holy sacrifice, acceptable to God, which is your spiritual service of worship.
And do not be conformed to this world, but be transformed by the renewing of your mind, so that you may prove what the will of God is, that which is good and acceptable and perfect. (Romans 12:1, 2 NASB)

God wants to prove His will through you, to you, and to those around you.
He loves you! Oh, how He loves you!

Our new nature fights with our old one. Or is it our old nature fights with our new one.
If our glass is half empty, we have a tendency to think that our old nature, which we believe to be inherently stronger, will defeat our weaker new nature. But if we believe our glass is half full, our new nature will always defeat the old one, especially when you top off the glass to running over with Jesus.

I think it's funny how the devil always talks us into believing our old nature is stronger than our new one. It's as if he tries to get us to dwell on our past old self, to get us to come into agreement with his future for us.

For though we walk in the flesh, we do not war according to the flesh, for the weapons of our warfare are not of the flesh, but divinely powerful for the destruction of fortresses. We are destroying speculations and every lofty thing raised up against the knowledge of God, and we are taking every thought captive to the obedience of Christ, and we are ready to punish all disobedience, whenever your obedience is complete. (2 Corinthians 10:3-6 NASB)

Perfect Is as Perfect Does...

He is Perfect — plans, timing, initiating to completion — He is Perfect. He is able to work perfectly within the bounds of our imperfections.

At the right time, Christ died for us. I would have picked right after Adam and Eve fell. But He didn't. He waited 4000 years, because His timing is perfect. His story of redemption is perfect.

His story for our lives is perfect as well. He is mindful that we are but dust, and yet completes a supernatural story for us and through us to His glory, as we trust Him. Even in imperfect trust.

Perfect is as Perfect does . . .

Let It Rain...

Bill Johnson says that Jesus changed everything. It didn't just rain on the righteous any longer, but by Him showing up in His majesty and grace, He declared it would rain on the righteous and unrighteous.

We can't work for salvation, and we can't work for rain. We simply get to trust Him for both, and receive both from Him by faith through grace.

Walk in the mud today, and rejoice in Him for your salvation.

Freedom Times 7000...

There is a freedom in Christ we read about, but may not walk in completely. I think it's available. All the promises of God are yes and amen.

There are over 7000 promises in the Word of God. They are all yes and amen. 7000 yeses and amen's! It would take just under two years if we took 10%, one promise of God a day, and believed it fully to completion in one day. Could you even imagine taking a promise in the morning, meditating on it, knowing it, and it accomplishing what it was sent forth to do in a day? Nope, we can't. Even though the Bible is packed full, and suddenly God moved. Even in the life of Jesus towards sinners, He is good to them, in that day. But to do the same and greater, as Jesus suggests (or is it commands?), is something that is for one day, sometime, in the future.

But nope, we have a vast array of promises that we know about, but won't walk in. Today is the day of salvation, but everything else, all the other promises are yes and wait. To borrow

Graham Cooke on another subject, "It is an invalid argument that makes us an invalid." Ask Him today for your promise. Today's the day . . . walk in the love of God's Word becoming reality in your life.

He Humbles Me Again...

"Papa, thank you for this beautiful sunrise, it's gorgeous!"

"David, I did it for you."

"How so, the sun comes up every day for everyone?"

"Because I knew eons ago, where you would be at the exact moment you would look up driving in from breakfast, see it, and appreciate it. So I can say I did it for you, because you are the only one from your perspective that could have seen it. You are the only one who could appreciate it. Those were your colors for you today. Since two physical objects can't exist in the exact same place at the same time, I did it for you. I love you. And thank you for taking the time to acknowledge Me, in what I took time to do for you."

"Thank you, Papa."

"Good morning, Papa. What's going on?"

"There is a fevered pitch of activity here. There is a great outpouring of My love that is about to take place in your area. People will try and classify it a revival or renewal, but it will simply be an outpouring of My love through My children. Decades of walls are about to fall, crumbling, and will not be rebuilt. Nothing can stand against My love. My love is going to pour out in words, deeds, and actions. What the intercessors a century ago were praying for will take place. And My children are going to sense My love for them and the lost more deeply. They will begin to and continue to see things from My perspective. In fact, the enemy will have his own vent page about Brownwood. I laugh at him because I see his day is coming."

"And you want me to post this?"

"Is there a reason you wouldn't?"

"No, Sir."

While driving up to Coleman, Texas, this morning, I watched a beautiful scissor-tail land on the back of a flying crow and peck the hound out of the back of its head, to drive it far from its nest.

for the weapons of our warfare are not of the flesh, but divinely powerful for the destruction of fortresses. (2 Corinthians 10:4 NASB)

Have a nice day, have fun fighting the devil!!!!!!

Is That a Mask?

Here is an interesting quote from a sermon. "Jesus came to put a face on God; we are here to put a face on Jesus."

So today (Halloween), as followers of Christ, how scary do we look to a lost world that needs a Savior?

ZZZ...

"David?"

"Papa?"

"David?"

"Papa?"

"David, the just shall live by faith. Not by what they produce, but by what I produce. I love you. Go back to sleep."

"Okay, love You. Thank You."

Contemplating on the greatness of God, needs to be mirrored by doing the greatness of God.

Truly, truly, I say to you, he who believes in Me, the works that I do, he will do also; and greater works than these he will do; because I go to the Father. (John 14:12 NASB)

He just ain't...

God isn't scared of us becoming everything Jesus is now and was on this earth.

Why should we be?

He triple God dares you to be like Jesus!!!!!

Here is a statement made by my dad about someone he witnessed to recently. "I've said all I can. It's up to the Holy Spirit to wise them up."

My dad is 87.

Holy Spirit, wise us up today!!!

Our significance can't be based on who we are, what we have, or what we don't have for that matter . . . Selah.

What makes us significant is having the Significant One, Jesus, flow through us, in His unlimited love, His unlimited grace, and His unlimited power.

What makes us significant is when the Significant One drips from us because of over flow, too much of Him for us to contain.

"David?"

"Yes, Papa?"

"David, a $5 bill is a help. A $20 bill is a blessing. A $100 bill makes a wonderful tract... Selah."

"Challenge yourself and others with this: take a $100 bill, and underline "In God We Trust." Then ask Me who, what random person, doesn't look at an outward appearance, or try and determine if they'll use the money correctly. Just go up and say, 'Merry Christmas, God loves you.' Don't preach, just bless them, and I'll start working on them. Have fun, I will!!!"

When you help someone out, don't think about how it looks. Just do it — quietly and unobtrusively. That is the way your God, who conceived you in love, working behind the scenes, helps you out. (Matthew 6:3-4 MSG)

Christmas not xmas...

The Christmas season is more than a celebration of Jesus' birth, although His birth is the paramount reason! It's a reminder of what can become of us without Him in our lives daily. Giving gifts and being charitable in this season is God's way of invading and softening even the hardest of hearts. It is a way of breaking complacency, and blowing the cob webs out of minds that have been inundated with the world for 11 months.

But what happens when we are complicit about complacency?

But realize this, that in the last days difficult times will come. For men will be lovers of self, lovers of money, boastful, arrogant, revilers, disobedient to parents, ungrateful, unholy, unloving, irreconcilable, malicious gossips, without self-control, brutal, haters of good, (2 Timothy 3:1-3 NASB)

Celebrate Jesus, the Gift of life!

You know it's Christmas...

You know, if we tore into Jesus, His power, His Word, and His promises, the way that kids tore into their presents yesterday, pushed His power, His Word, and His promises to the max to see what they can do like kids do with their toys, we'd probably be living in a different world today! I know you worked hard all year, listened to conversations, or saw what got their attention on TV. You bought their requests, stayed up all night assembling and wrapping, waiting in anticipation to see the excitement on their faces when they saw all the presents.

The Father is the same way, waiting in anticipation to see the excitement of you when you encounter Jesus. It cost Him a lot. He wrapped Him in an earth suit and waited 30 years to watch His present to mankind take full advantage of Himself. He destroyed the power of the enemy by healing and doing miracles, took the keys of death and hell, laid down beside Him — all so we could operate the same way.

"Okay, Papa, show us what You want done or said today. It's the day after Christmas and we've got toys You gave us. And if something doesn't work right we'll read the instruction manual!!!!!"

Breaking the Power of Broken Resolutions...

Ask God what resolutions, IF ANY, you need to make. Then dissolve your resolve to make it happen on your own, and let Him do it through you. Better yet, with the principle of doing things in secret as in Matthew 6, keep your list, IF ANY, between you and Him SECRET. Rely on Him to keep you accountable, and not your list of accountability partners that you'll end up disappointing and avoiding. Selah

It's not I who lives, but Christ who lives in me.

It's not I who diets, but Christ who diets in me.
It's not I who is more disciplined, but it's Christ who is disciplined in me.
It's not I who runs, but Christ who runs in me.
It's not I who doesn't gossip, but Christ who doesn't gossip in me. Etc.

Living a life based on our own will power sucks. Living a life with Christ living through us doesn't.

You are more like Jesus than you think you are. Set Him loose in your life.

Piggyback...

Holiness isn't what we do, it's who we are because of Who lives in us. How can we become more holy than Christ Jesus who dwells in us? To "be holy" we don't have to stop anything or start anything. We simply let Him live through us. If our sins are forgiven — past, present and future — because of the blood of Christ, then we are seen as holy. . . past, present and future.

Cease striving to be holy. It only empowers the law that Christ died to fulfill. We can't make our own way. He made it for us. Enjoy the piggy back ride. He's got you; He's done all the work for you. Hold on tight!!!

Obtain, Maintain...

"David?"

"Yes, Papa?"

"David, you can only obtain holiness through what Jesus did."

"David?"

"Yes, Papa?"

"David, you can only maintain holiness through what Jesus is doing in you today. I love you."
"Love you too, Papa. Thank you."

"Papa?"

"Yes, David?"

"That takes a load off."

"It was meant to. Love you again."

"Papa?"

"Yes, David?"

"I want You to have everything You need from me, and want from me."

"Okay, I'll take it. And thank you."

"So here's what I want you to do. With God helping you: take your everyday, ordinary life — your sleeping, eating, going-to-work, and walking-around life — and place it before God as an offering. Embracing what God does for you is the best thing you can do for Him. Don't become so well-adjusted to your culture that you fit into it without even thinking. Instead, fix your attention on God. You'll be changed from the inside out. Readily recognize what he wants from you, and quickly respond to it. Unlike the culture around you, always dragging you down to its level of immaturity, God brings the best out of you, and develops well-formed maturity in you." (Romans 12:1, 2 MSG)

Jesus Digs His Digs!

We are the workmanship of God, the temples as believers in Christ, made with His hands so He could dwell in us.

David saw this, I believe, when he looked around at the tabernacle, a tent made by man according to God's instruction, with golden elements to aid in worship of God, and a golden covered ark with Cherubim on top. It was made to exact specifications, but it was Who dwelt there that made it lovely.

Consider this . . . you're lovely!

David wrote:
How lovely are Your dwelling places, O Lord of hosts! (Psalms 84:1 NASB)

You're lovely . . . made to His exact specifications so He could dwell in you because of His Son's death, burial, and resurrection. You're lovely because He dwells in you. You're quite the abode for the Father, Son, and Holy Spirit to abide in!!!! Jesus digs His digs!

Cut to the Quick: the Heart...

He again fixes a certain day, "today," saying through David after so long a time, just as has been said before,
"Today if you hear His voice, Do not harden your hearts." (Hebrews 4:7 NASB)

In Acts 2:14-38, Peter preached an incredible sermon and the people within hearing distance were cut to the quick and repented. About 3000 souls were added that day.

A few years later in Acts 7, Stephen, a man full of the Holy Ghost, had a similar circumstance. He preached a verbal treatise and history of Israel, and testified of Christ Jesus. Those folks were cut to the quick as well, but instead of being saved, they stoned Stephen.

The point is, when we speak under the unction of the Holy Spirit — SPEAK — the quickening that happens in people's hearts will not always go the way we think. In Acts 2, 3000 got saved. But in Acts 7, the coats of the people that stoned Stephen were laid at the feet of a future Apostle, writer of two thirds of the New Testament. Speak what He tells us to speak. We will never know what His outcome will be, but lives will be changed for His glory!!!!

Such a Character...

The toughest place to build character is in the middle of God's abundant blessings, not in the lack . . .

WHATEVER?!!!!

The hopefulness in Jesus is the only thing that can confront and abolish the hopelessness of the world. The Prince of Peace breaks down walls and envelops us with a peace that passes all human understanding, even guarding our heart and mind in Him. So what is our mind going to dwell on then? Whatever?!!!

Finally, brethren, whatever is true, whatever is honorable, whatever is right, whatever is pure, whatever is lovely, whatever is of good repute, if there is any excellence and if anything worthy of praise, dwell on these things. (Philippians 4:8 NASB)

Milk Mustache, the Sign of Fullness ...

Think of a child who is given a full glass of milk by his dad, but the child only takes a sip. It's bought, paid for, and there's plenty more where it came from. But because he thinks he's only worthy of a sip, that's all he takes. He is holding fullness in his hand, but won't dare partake of it, all because of his mindset, not his dad's. If his dad wanted him to have only a sip, he would have poured him only a sip.

At times, I hear people say, "I don't deserve God's grace." Yes, we all deserve his grace. That's why Jesus died. We deserve God's grace because of what Jesus did, not because of what we've done. He died to give us grace, because we couldn't earn it. We are valuable enough to Him, for Him to die for us. If we say we don't deserve His grace, how will we ever operate in the fullness of it?

Favor is not earned, it is grown into. Jesus grew in favor with God and man. We cannot earn that which is freely given.

Drink fully that which He has given you! You look awesome in that mustache!!!!!

A Day Without Regret...

Note to self: don't think about now what I wanted to do for The Lord yesterday. But keep up with the pace of Heaven to do yesterday, what I can remember wonderfully now!!!!!

Merry Christmas to all, and God bless us, every one!

This May Be a Bit Convoluted But...

There is a truism, that those of us who say that God is too busy to deal with us or our problems, or that they're too small a problem, are probably:
1. too busy to be dealt with,
2. stay busy because anything else would unmask the pain (and Who, including God wants to go there) of letting our problems be dealt with,
3. too small in our thinking to know that the Creator of the universe cares that much about the mundane or painful areas in our lives.

He wants to deal with the small things in our lives, so in turn He can show us the small things in peoples' lives and reinvest what He has given us to change people.

A smile with Jesus behind it is a terrible thing to waste. Give today!!!!!!

Nothing is too small or too unimportant to Him.

Draw near to God and He will draw near to you.

Childish or Childlike?

In order for us to become more childlike, we must put away childish things. But I think the more we engage God as adults, the more we disengage ourselves from heaven's perspective. God is not interested in our opinion of heaven as much as He is interested in heaven's opinion of us. Stay in the Word, and don't be scared to ask Him.

and said, "Truly I say to you, unless you are converted and become like children, you will not enter the kingdom of heaven. (Matthew 18:3 NASB)

Truly I say to you, whoever does not receive the kingdom of God like a child will not enter it at all. " (Mark 10:15 NASB)

God Waxes...

He is Omnipotent, all powerful!!!

The mountains melted like wax at the presence of the LORD, At the presence of the Lord of the whole earth. (Psalms 97:5 NASB)

Now that's power!!!! His presence melts mountains like wax! And we are constantly asking Him, "Give us all You have!!!" Think of all the power facets of the All Powerful God — His love, His grace, His mercy, the Blood, healing, miracles, His presence, His judgment, His creative power, His destructive power, His humility!!!

I know, I know. But I've got to say it . . . with great power comes great responsibility!!! That's why the All Powerful is also the All Knowing, and because the Ever Present is in us and around us, we have access to all of Him at any given moment. He gives us, through Jesus, the ability to act like His Son, by the power of His Spirit. Stepping into His presence, YOUR mountains melt like wax!!!

Have you waxed today? He's ready!!!

Are you in the will...?

God doesn't want you doing what's easy for you, and He doesn't want you doing what's hard for you. He simply wants you doing what's good for you. If something is hard, good!!!! That means, you WILL (by an active choosing of your will) let God's grace pour through you to carry you through hard events in life. If what you are doing is easy, LET His grace . . . again an active choice of your will, carry you further than you ever thought possible. If you always choose, by an act of your will, the grace side of things, you will line up with His will. Two wills, natural and Providential, headed in the same direction — hard to beat and hard to stop!

The Strength of Vulnerability...

We can strengthen ourselves physically, we can strengthen ourselves emotionally, and we can, through shrewd investment, strengthen ourselves financially. But to strengthen ourselves spiritually, we have to become most vulnerable, to the point of being childlike (not childish). Childlike in the sense and awe that we can do nothing on our own, nothing on our own initiative, but like Jesus, trust the Father completely!! God exalts the humble and resists the proud . . .

and said to them, "Whoever receives this child in My name receives Me, and whoever receives Me receives Him who sent Me; for the one who is least among all of you, this is the one who is great." (Luke 9:48 NASB)

First Things First...

Be assured that from the first day we heard of you, we haven't stopped praying for you, asking God to give you wise minds and spirits attuned to his will, and so acquire a thorough understanding of the ways in which God works. We pray that you'll live well for the Master, making him proud of you as you work hard in his orchard. As you learn more and more how God works, you will learn how to do your work. We pray that you'll have the strength to stick it out over the long haul — not the grim strength of gritting your teeth but the glory-strength God gives. It is strength that endures the unendurable and spills over into joy, thanking the Father who makes us strong enough to take part in everything bright and beautiful that he has for us. (Colossians 1:9-12 MSG)

Scrambled Thoughts, Rather Than Eggs

Too many Jesus movies . . . There is no audible thematic background movie music in real life in our walk with Christ.

I think our inaction as believers is based on NOT feeling something at times. As if we wait for mood music to start. Then we pray, or wait for the crescendo, knowing that there's a big finish up ahead, after ". . . in Jesus name. Amen."

Think about Jesus' day, walking and dodging smelly donkey, camel, cow poop. There was the din of large crowds following Him, snooty scribes, fake Pharisees watching, weighing everything He said and did. That didn't stop the Son of Man demonstrating He was the Son of God. Jesus didn't wait for mood music, there was no panning cameras catching the crowds' reactions, no reality TV cameras recording every moment of His life. There was no 'boom-chicka-wow-woooow' music when He looked at the woman caught in adultery. But the music . . . NO! . . . The Opus No. 1 of forgiveness and grace was playing!

He walked this Earth as a man, leaving His divinity in heaven, taking up our humanity, dying and shedding His blood for us, to give us the grace to lay down our humanity and pick up His divinity, so we can do the same as He did and more!!!! Our segue is from glory to glory, living His design through us. But He does sing over us, and there is no earthly composer that can match that!!!! Our life in Him is the music . . .

What are we co-composing with Him today?!!!

I've Been Made...

You know, over the years I've heard people say, "Wow, if you make this amount of money, or own your own house and be debt free, you'll have it made."

All I know, is when I asked Jesus in my heart, that started my making, and when I hear from my Master...

Well done, good and faithful slave. You were faithful with a few things, I will put you in charge of many things; enter into the joy of your master.' (Matthew 25:21 NASB)

Then will I have it made.

Happy Thanksgiving ...
God's Name is Terrible!

I've listened to some of the anti-God pundits, not all, but some. And I've come to the conclusion that they are merely exposing their own hearts and character, not His.

"Well, if God is such a loving God, why does He let children starve in Africa?" (I was actually asked that question in Chiropractic College.)

I responded with, "What are you doing about it?" God does His work through people, righteous and unrighteous. Look at Psalm 99:3 in the KJV ...
Let them praise thy great and terrible name; for it is holy. (Psalm 99:3 KJV)

Imagine us standing before an all consuming holy and infinitely loving God. As we stand in His presence, at the speed of thought, we realize just how wonderful, incredible, all consuming, and loving is His nature and character. And what a terrible nature we have, how we have failed Him, time and time again. We cry out that He is Holy, and at His name our own selfishness, self-centeredness, hateful, and despising nature is exposed. Yes, His name is terrible, because it exposes our true nature as we stand before Him!!!

So, what part of God's work are we actually doing? If we say God doesn't feed the poor, we condemn ourselves. Let's be doers of the Word and not just hearers, or worse yet, accusers of the Holy One. Oh, and the only way to escape the terrible Day of Judgment? Ask the Lord Jesus to live in you and change you!!

Dear David,

In regard to your last petition, yes, I will heal a dog. Yes, I will provide for that family in need. Yes, I will restore that person's soul, and they will return to their first love. In fact, all my promises are yes and amen.

I appreciate you making your requests and petitions with thanksgiving according to My Word. However, the formality in which you make them is unnecessary, since I already know what you're in need of. Kindly refrain from the religious tone post haste, and come, sup with Me at anytime.

Kindest regards,

Jesus
Lover of your soul.

Can You Fix This?

If we are fixated on fixing ourselves we are fixin' to feel a world of disappointment. Fix our eyes upon Jesus, and let Him fixate on us His way, His order, His results, His glory!!!!!

Luke 5 ... The Fish Lotto

And He got into one of the boats, which was Simon's, and asked him to put out a little way from the land. And He sat down and began teaching the people from the boat. When He had finished speaking, He said to Simon, "Put out into the deep water and let down your nets for a catch." Simon answered and said, "Master, we worked hard all night and caught nothing, but I will do as You say and let down the nets." When they had done this, they enclosed a great quantity of fish, and their nets began to break; so they signaled to their partners in the other boat for them to come and help them. And they came and filled both of the boats, so that they began to sink. But when Simon Peter saw that, he fell down at Jesus' feet, saying, "Go away from me Lord, for I am a sinful man!" For amazement had seized him and all his companions because of the catch of fish which they had taken;
(Luke 5:3-9 NASB)

Sometimes Jesus puts us in a position of trusting Him in the same area we have failed, trudged along, and settled within ourselves, saying "what's the use . . ."

Then miraculously He takes our offering, like the use of Peters boat in Luke 5, even with the attitude that Peter has, "I've done all this, Lord, but just because you asked, I'll do it." And then suddenly God moves. Peter is blessed beyond what his boat can hold, and has to call another boat to help carry the load of fish. Jesus can bless you in a moment of what you think is a fruitless endeavor. And we can walk away like Peter, knowing Who the Lord is and Who is Lord of all creation, and smelling like an abundance of fish!!!

Let us not lose heart in doing good, for in due time we will reap if we do not grow weary. (Galatians 6:9 NASB)

Lava Lamp Prayer...

I was watching a Lava Lamp a while back just as it was turned on. There was a light that caused the 'lava' to glow. I touched the glass vessel and it was cool. I grabbed some coffee, sat and watched, especially after the Lord said, "Watch this." There is a lesson involved when He says that.

After several minutes the lava surface began to swell upwards and then shrink back. I saw, after several more minutes, an ebb and flow. Then one bubble broke loose and went half way up, then another, and another. Finally, one went to the narrow top, cooled, and came back down. I touched the glass. It was warmer. I sat back, slowly finishing my coffee and watching. The process sped up and it was fun to watch the boiling lava rising, then the cooling and falling. Beautiful lucid patterns were before me.

The Lord said, "David, this is how prayer is. Sometimes it's a lot of work at first, heating up a cooled prayer life, seemingly unanswered. But you ask and keep on asking, seek and keep on seeking, knock and keep on knocking 'till the door falls down! This is why I say pray continuously. When a prayer seems to go up half way, and falls unanswered, don't give up . . . keep going! The light is the willingness to pray, the lava is the faith, the substance hoped for, getting to the top. The coolness, once there, gently falls back, answered. Keep praying."

Rejoice always; pray without ceasing; in everything give thanks; for this is God's will for you in Christ Jesus. Do not quench the Spirit; do not despise prophetic utterances. But examine everything carefully; hold fast to that which is good; abstain from every form of evil. (1 Thessalonians 5:16-22 NASB)

Persistence is the Key to Persistence.

There are changes the Lord desires to do in us. It's His persistence that's key in our persistence to see those changes made. It's not our faith. He gave us a measure of faith first, but it's not our iron will that accomplishes things, it's His will. We get in line and that flow causes us to persevere.

With what severity are we going to persevere? Don't quit, keep going, and allow character to be proved. God knows you have it in you because He's in you. YOU don't know what you have in you, until God pressurizes life, and He explodes through you.

Pursue and over take, persist in persistence, and get severe in perseverance!

Graciousness Is Spaciousness...

How big does God's grace impact your life? Is He there just to save you and you got the rest? Is He there for you four and no more? Is there a grace for cutting up carrots? I know there's one for dirty diapers. But is there one for bad report cards? Do you have a grace for sharing a couple of extra bucks with a guy walking the street? Do you allow God's grace into every area of your life?

Do you have a..."I can't sleep. I don't know why I'm going to the grocery store at one in the morning and end up letting a checker or stocker unload on you emotionally for five minutes. They don't know why they're telling me this, but somehow they feel better,"... grace?

Grace is about extending part of God's life for you into someone else's, to hopefully make room, if they don't know Him. Not just room, but a Grace Space in the Kingdom.

Ohhhh, wow! It's... it's like you... you know, that... that... that... you're like... you know, so spaced out on grace. It's like... like... you know... like a high! It's like... exemplar to be sooooo heavenly minded, that you end up earthly good.

Use the grace God has given you, there's always space for one more in His Kingdom.

R-E-S-P-E-C-T

. . .yet, with respect to the promise of God, he did not waver in unbelief but grew strong in faith, giving glory to God, and being fully assured that what God had promised, He was able also to perform. Therefore, it was also credited to him as righteousness.
(Romans 4:20-22 NASB)

How do we not waver in unbelief?

We respect what God promises.

How do we grow strong in faith?

We respect what God promises.

How do we glory in God, and be fully assured that He's able to perform?

We respect what God promises.

But the key to "respect" is the preceding 3 letter word, Y-E-T.
No matter how crazy . . . YET
No matter how impossible . . . YET
No matter what the circumstances . . . YET!
Yet, with respect to God's promises . . .

...And It Was Credited to Him as Righteousness.

Do we respect God's promises to us to set a precedent of righteousness like He did with Abraham? Let's do so!!

Can I See Some I.D.?

Jesus didn't come to earth to reinforce our identity as sinners, but to reinforce our identity as children of the Most High. We are called as agents, to the greatest adoption agency in the universe.

He didn't come here as the Son of God to show us how we can't, but as the Son of Man to show us how we can!

Fear this...

The fear of man is a deadly trap. It precludes us from a deepening relationship with God. And yet the proverb, "A good name is better to have than riches," tells us to walk our life in such a way that we need to value man's opinion of ourselves as well. We can't do that though, without the guidance of the Holy Spirit, and by stepping into the footsteps of His Grace.

The fear of God is the beginning of wisdom. The fear of man is the end of it.

Trust Him with your walk today.

Grave Image...

You know, you would have figured someone who died for you would be more controlling or demanding, because of their sacrifice. Like someone trying to control you from the grave. But that's not His way. He laid it all out freely, as a free will offering. In fact, the fact He's not in the grave has liberated us to freely engage in a relationship. Is He holy? Yes. Is He righteous, truthful and just? Yes. He is everything we need in this life to become as He is.

He had a grave experience to bring us and complete us, in His image. So thankful for His life, His shed blood, death, burial and resurrection.

Our life doesn't have to be grave, because He emptied it.

It's Not All the Time, BUT...

I think apologetics is the gathering of "Holy Spirit inspired answers" to age old questions that eventually make good arguments. We are to study to show ourselves approved, but if we completely rely on old arguments we may miss out on what the Holy Spirit wants to do in the here and now with the person in front of us. Our testimony is, I believe, to inspire others to greater intimacy with Him.

Apologetics though aren't like cartoon guns that never run out if bullets. We will run out of arguments. If we use apologetics to argue with people, we always have the finishing blow waiting in the back of our mind to abolish the other person's argument. But we may miss the opportunity to hear them, and be quickened in the moment by the Holy Spirit. We're more impressed with what we have to say than with what they're saying, and more impressed with our logic than God's ever present current answer to that person's need.

Let's listen the way He listens, and respond the way He wants, with nothing on our own initiative . . . like Jesus.

It's His Bragging Rights, Not Ours...

For by grace you have been saved through faith; and that not of yourselves, it is the gift of God; not as a result of works, so that no one may boast. (Ephesians 2:8, 9 NASB)

We have, after salvation, found ourselves at times boasting in our works. Isn't it funny how it's His grace that gets us saved, it is His grace which works through us, but we'll take credit for that which didn't even originate with us?

We are co-heirs, co-laborers. Me thinks though, we need to be co-humiliters (if there is such a word), where we focus on being humble as He is humble, so His grace flows through us to accomplish all He has for us to accomplish. And our boasting always turns to Him.

Here, Hold My crown, and Watch This...

To re-ceive is important in our walk with Christ. To ceive is to catch, or hold on to. To re-ceive is to re catch or take hold of again. So let go of whatever you're believing God for, throw it out there, let Him have it, He'll throw it back.

There nothing like playing catch with your Dad!!!!!

Pretty Dry Here, Wonder What It's Like Over Yonder?

God makes a home for the lonely; He leads out the prisoners into prosperity, Only the rebellious dwell in a parched land. (Psalms 68:6 NASB)

The reason we need courage, is because we are free moral beings. If we were God's robots, we wouldn't need courage. God has boldness, strength, and courage available to us. It is as vast as His love is towards us. God's love is bold, courageous, and strong. We can walk in boldness, courage, and strength everyday as we walk in His grace. It's not just for times of trouble.

End Credits...

"So, Papa, wanna watch a movie?"

"Yes, Die Hard, the first one. I want to show you something."

"Okay, done..."

"The enemy wants you dead... wants to destroy those you love. The "good guys" may not understand what your situation is. They will end up giving you no help, and actually helping the enemy. Don't give up. You will win."

Hello...?

"Lord, I'm not hearing too much from You..."

"Have you tried talking with Me and not at Me?"

"Has been kinda one sided, hasn't it?"

"Let's just say your use of commas has been extensive. But I think a fermata is more accurate, since you've been conducting these talks."

"Papa, what do YOU want to talk about?"

"Glad you asked. How about I hold the baton a while, hmm?"

And One and Two and . . .

You know, there's just something about the Lord singing, "David, David, I love you! David, David, I love you! David, David, I love you! Daaaaavid, David, I love you!" to the William Tell Overture (Lone Ranger Theme). That just puts a spring in my step!!!!!

What's He singing over you today?!

Hungry?!!!!

Looking forward to some great Holiday food!!!!!

Jesus said to them, "My food is to do the will of Him who sent Me and to accomplish His work. (John 4:34 NASB)

The Kingdom has an incredibly rich diet!!!

He Humbles Himself Again.

Last night, the Lord kept telling me as we were taking communion, "Thank you, for honoring Me. Thank you, for honoring Me."

I am always amazed at the Lord's humility. He is the most powerful, humble being in the universe.

You're so classy...

Gloria Steinem once said, "Planning ahead is a measure of class. The rich and even the middle class plan for future generations, but the poor can plan ahead only a few weeks or days."

A good man leaves an inheritance to his children's children, And the wealth of the sinner is stored up for the righteous. (Proverbs 13:22 NASB)

Simple as building blocks...

God has given you the ability to structure your day by hearing His voice. He orders the steps of the righteous.

Jesus, The Ultimate Make Over...

"To understand Heaven's actual language, David, you have to be here. No human can understand the depth and beauty of Our language here. So We translate that into action, or works, as James puts it, so you can comprehend Our language on Earth."

"We could never talk to you all enough, not even an eternity, to get you to understand how much you all are really deeply, richly, and completely loved. I had to demonstrate Our language of Heaven through Jesus."

"Jesus wasn't just a carpenter. He was a repairer of broken down, dilapidated temples that I built out of love. But He couldn't just talk with them to fix them; He demonstrated Our love in incredibly wonderful ways. It wasn't just words that got Jesus killed, it was His heaven to earth actions, too. No one could refute the actions so they lied about what He said. He demonstrated Our love for mankind through His death, burial, resurrection and ascension."

"So I say all of this to tell you, 'We need more of heaven's actions through you and others, who are willing to take heavenly words, guided by the Spirit, and demonstrate Our love into action to help restore the temples I created.'"

Jesus is the ultimate Make Over. Follow in His footsteps, be led the same as He was, and do the same and greater! You have permission!

"David?"

"Yes, Papa?"

"You keep pulling on parts of Me to strengthen your weak areas, to bring them into balance with your strong areas. Pull on all of Me, to make your weak areas stronger, and your strong areas MEEKER. The meek inherit the earth."

"Makes all the sense in the world, now. Thank you, my Papa!!!"

"David?"

"Yes . . . (Stretch . . . yawn), Papa?"

"Believers everywhere are turned and focused on Me, facing Me. I need them to turn around and go out. I live in them, I abide in them, I'm not going anywhere without them, but they aren't going anywhere at all. Talk to a straggler today. Talk to fringes today. The Good Shepherd leaves the ninety-nine to find the one. That's actually a model for every believer, and not just the pastor. Listen to some Fringies today, let them talk, listen and point them back to the Good Shepherd. There are a lot of good sheep on the fringe. I'll give believers wisdom as they ask to minister to the Fringies! Love you, David."

"Love you, too!!!! Thank you. Is Fringies like a heavenly term?"

"David?"

"Yes, Sir."

"You can sleep 30 more minutes . . ."

"You sure?"

"Yes, I'm sure . . . I run the universe."

(After 30 minutes)
"David?"

"Yes, Papa?"

"Love births obedience, love maintains obedience, love completes obedience! Love releases obedience, obedience doesn't release love. Jesus went to the cross out of complete love for Me and you. It wasn't a focused iron will of His own that caused Him to die. He was a complete and total manifestation of My love towards man, even to the point of death. He died to bring a completeness of love between man and Myself. Yes, you are crucified with Him, buried with Him, and have a new life in Him out of love, not an über discipline. Savvy?"

"Oui. Danke, Papa!!!!"

"The more humble one stays at God's feet, the more useful he is in God's hand."

Watchman Nee

Fearing the Fear...

One part of our life as a Christian isn't about not being fearful. Being fearful of being fearful is still fear. Christ's love for us and through us addresses our ability to work in the midst of the most fearful circumstances, our own and that of others. Love conquers all!!!! Again, the best way to keep your knees from knocking is to take a step forward!

A Bit Long Today...

I got very badly sunburned day before yesterday. So much so, the end of my nose is seeping serous fluid. The Lord woke me up in the middle of the night and said to put on the after tanning lotion. I told Him I don't like lotion on and sleeping, don't like how it feels, sticky and all. He said, "You're really not going to like how you feel if you don't." He was right of course; stinging is down about half now.

Then we had a talk based on how obedience isn't based on how I feel, but it's based on how I feel about Him. Funny how He dressed me down in a most pleasant and loving way!!!!

I wanted to be in the Marines, I tried to join, but because of a football injury, I was permanently disqualified from any military service. I was very disappointed, and always felt I needed the discipline in my life. Even after the Lord told me He had a different boot camp, a different and better way to bring discipline to my life (which He has), I still resented not serving my country. A couple of years back, after reminding the Lord of my resentment, He simply told me if I had gone in, I'd be dead. At that time it was the beginning of Desert Shield. He said that He needed me to serve His Kingdom rather than my country.

My point being, sometimes WE feel as if we need a drill instructor, hollering in our ear, to get us to do something, because we think it's the harshness of God, not the kindness of God, that leads to repentance. Selah

All I know is, after 30 years of an intimate walk with Him, the stronger I feel He needs to be with me by dressing me down, the more gentle His voice becomes.

It's funny how we project our own warped and crooked humanity on Him, vetting against Him with our own self righteousness, as filthy as it is. All the while, He wants to infuse a loving relationship on us through Jesus' blood by the finished work of the Cross, to the newness of an intimate relationship with the Holy Spirit.

The voice of him that crieth in the wilderness, Prepare ye the way of the Lord, make straight in the desert a highway for our God. Every valley shall be exalted, and every mountain and hill shall be made low: and the crooked shall be made straight, and the rough places plain: and the glory of the Lord shall be revealed, and all flesh shall see it together: for the mouth of the Lord hath spoken it. (Isaiah 40:3-5 KJV)

"David?"

"Yes, Papa?"

"Sometimes the valley you're walking through is not yours, but someone else's. Stay available. You may be the only Sherpa they have to guide them through, and to help carry the load. Let the Holy Spirit be y'all's GPS. Love you!!!"

"Love you, too!!!"

Something I Learned While Playing Golf with Heath, My Son-in-Law.

"David?"

"Yes, Papa?"

"Keep your head down and have fun." (Swing, missed it. Swing and topped it.)

"David..."

"Yes, Papa?"

"Keep your head down and have fun." (Swing and a shank...)

"David..."

"Yes, Papa, I know. 'Keep your head down and have fun.'" (Swing and a hook...)

"David?"

"You know, Papa, this is why I gave up the game!!!"

"David, do you see your swing in your head?"

"Yes."

"Do you see where the ball wants to go?"

"Yes."

"Well, golf is like a life of faith. Sometime folks get so excited on where they're going, that they don't concentrate on what's in front of them. They are constantly pulling their head up, seeing if they made it, and missing the point of contact. Or they forget to have fun because, 'This is serious.' They put themselves under so much pressure to perform, that everything becomes rigid and tight. So keep your head down, relax, and have fun."

"Okay . . . (Swing and smack) that's easy . . . Thank you, Papa!!!!"

"Yes, David, like that. And I like 12, 12 tribes, 12 apostles, 12 on this hole . . ."

"Oh and You keep score too . . ."

More Golf...

The Lord showed me an interesting parallel in golf. Getting the ball in the cup is the completion of our desire. The ball is our point of contact, it could be a Bible verse, a person we want to see helped, a situation changed. But it's His take on what is used as a club that I found interesting.

He explained that some people use Him as a club, thinking how can you go wrong USING God to get to your end result? How can you hit a shank shot with God as your club, right? And the crazy thing to me is that God will let us do that to prove a point, to show that even USING God we can still hit a shank shot. The other point is where we say, "I only want to be used by God," and God allows us to be used as a club in His hands, just to show He can wear us out, and exhaust us. But that is not His design for us either, I believe.

The club we are to use is faith. The goal in golf is to get the ball into the hole in as few strokes as possible. (Thank you, Harvey Penick, for that bit of advice.) God's desire is to walk with us and teach us how to use different clubs of faith for different situations. We might need a driving faith or an easy faith to lob the ball on the green. All the clubs are important, but all the clubs aren't used on every hole — only about three or four. Sometimes the putter is not used at all. Woohoo! The fruits of the Spirit are there to help us in our game: patience, kindness, joy, etc. The gifts of the Spirit are those cool tools that God gives us to help us complete the game against a very wary opponent.

Keep your head down, relax and have fun.

"David . . ."

"Yes, sir?"

"Man can neither quantify nor qualify humility. Only I can see into a man's heart. Yes, man can see the fruit, and make a call on whether someone is humble or not."

"My question for you is this; what would appear more humble to man? One who is quick to repent before Me after they have sinned, or one who lives their life before Me with no need to repent? I say man would see the repentant man more humble, and the no-need-for-repentance man as "holier than thou." How do I know this? I lived that life on earth, through My Son."

"One who walks in humility stays in a state of repentance, always focused on Me. One who is constantly repenting hasn't fully grasped the work on the Cross, or the emptying of a rich man's tomb. Selah. I want them repenting, make no mistake, but I want them walking in humility rather than always needing to be humbled."

"Remember what I have told you before. If you are humiliated, it's a pride issue inside you. If you are humbled, you are headed in the right direction, but you looked right or left. Keep your eyes upon Me."

"So helpful, Papa!! Thank you!!!!"

Does This Make Sense?

The prodigal son wasn't prodigal until he spent his inheritance. He could've saved every last dime of his inheritance, left, and still broken fellowship with his father. He would've returned as the selfish frugal son.

The word prodigal means to spend lavishly. Can we be prodigals for the Kingdom, spending lavishly what our Father gives us on a lost and dying generation?! Not just resources, but spending lavishly our love, our prayers, healing. Can we be prodigals for His kingdom?

"Silver and gold I have none, but what I do have I give to you. In the Name of Jesus the Nazarene, arise and walk!"

Favor (from Graham Cooke's Favor series)

I am blessed with the unparalleled, unmerited favor of the Lord.

Favor is a shield around me.

I am growing in favor, with God and man.

I am favored everywhere I go, at home, in the workplace, at church, in my relationships and in my walk with God.

I am favored in all that I do; doors of opportunity will open for me. Blessings are attracted to me. Increase upon increase will flow towards me.

I proclaim that I am in training for reigning.

My favor trains me to receive, and I will develop the life that God has set aside for me in Christ. Nothing shall prevent me from completing my training in favor.

I joyfully give myself wholeheartedly for becoming a person of absolute favor in the Holy Spirit.

In Jesus name, amen!

"David . . ."

"Yes, Papa?"

"You have favor, and you walk in favor. You have so much favor, you're part of a tribe."

"A tribe?"

"Yes, the FAVOR-ites!!!"

He's Everything He's Cracked Up to Be ...

Let's face it. Jesus is sometimes like going to the chiropractor. We have an area that is adhered, we have a loss of freedom of motion in Him, but we avoid the pain of having the adhesion broken because it HURTS!

So you go to Him anticipating the pain of tearing adhesion. He lays hands on you. Virtue, instead of pain pours from His hands. Love, grace, and mercy flows through us from Him and the adhesion melts under His loving hands. Our freedom is restored.

But really, let's face it. Jesus really is like going to Jesus!!!

Kings and Priests...

We are not an "heir apparent." We are not a person who will inherit a title or position when someone dies. We are co-heirs with the King, Christ, because He lives! We have all the rights, privileges, and heavenly authority He has given us to be majestic ambassadors for Him.

Proclaiming His love, and demonstrating His love through our actions, signs, wonders, deeds and words, let us walk in the same manner of grace, mercy, and compassion He did. Let Him show off His majesty in you!!!!! Be available to demonstrate why He is a good King!!!!

"David?"

"Papa?"

"Life, like golf, needs to be deliberate. Remember the folks you were watching on the driving range a while back?"

"Yes, Sir."

"You watched one man who hit every range ball like it was 'the' shot he had to make. He would move a ball into position, stand behind it, access his shot, address the ball for a practice swing, take a practice swing, address the ball again, and then swing. The ball landed close to where he wanted it. Why were you impressed?"

"Because he was pitching the ball about 10 yards away to a pin, and there was an 8 foot tall net between him and the pin. He just pitched the ball about four feet over the net . . . every time around the pin."

"What was happening on some other tees?"

"One guy had a large bucket of balls, and was hitting them. But he seemed more determined to finish the bucket of balls than really working on where the balls were going. Also, the other man who was more deliberate in practice had a smaller bucket of balls."

"Yes, that's right. Because he was more deliberate in what he was doing, he spent less time more effectively. Instead of hitting a large bucket of balls as hard and fast as he could, he wasn't frustrated and enjoyed hitting a smaller one. I know what you're thinking . . . 'being that deliberate could lead to legalism.' Being deliberate, David, in Me, being deliberate flowing in My Spirit, being deliberate in relationship with Me makes legalism very unattractive. I made it that way deliberately. I love you."

"And I love You. Thank You!!!"

Maintaining Freedom...

There is a freedom in Christ that comes from none other than spending time with Him. He is Victor over your victim circumstances, and He is the Great Liberator. Put your "stuff" in front of Him and let Him look at it. Then let Him look at you, and you look at Him, " . . . and watch how things of this earth will grow strangely dim." I'm not saying that I have this all together, that I have it made. But I am well on my way, reaching out for Christ, who has so wondrously reached out for me. Friends, don't get me wrong: by no means do I count myself an expert in all of this. But I've got my eye on the goal, where God is beckoning us onward — to Jesus. I'm off and running and I'm not turning back.

So let's keep focused on that goal, those of us who want everything God has for us. If any of you have something else in mind, something less than total commitment, God will clear your blurred vision — you'll see it yet! Now that we're on the right track, let's stay on it. (Philippians 3:12-16 MSG)

He Broadcasts 24/7/Eternal ...

We are so bombarded with external noises, that I think we forget we have to attenuate, tune in from the inside. The enemy loves the external pressure of the spirit of the world to draw us away from Who lives inside us. "Greater is He Who is in you, than He that's in the world." His signal radiates on the inside of us to undo and undermine the enemy's broadcast. He broadcasts His voice 24/7/Eternal . . . to His children and the lost.

Stop, listen, and tune in on His signal. It is stronger than the enemy's. Turn and follow that voice. It will lead you, guide you, and help you to walk in the ordered steps of your life!!!

I've never known kindness not to eventually work . . .

6. and raised us up with Him, and seated us with Him in the heavenly places in Christ Jesus,
7. so that in the AGES to come He might SHOW the surpassing riches of His grace in KINDNESS toward us in Christ Jesus.
8. For by grace you have been saved through faith; and that not of yourselves, it is the gift of God;
9. not as a result of works, so that no one may boast.
10. For we are His workmanship, created in Christ Jesus for good works, which God prepared beforehand so that we would walk in them. (Ephesians 2:6-10 NASB)

We are in one of the ages to come!!! How has He shown the surpassing richness of His grace in kindness through us this week — and if not this week, how about today? It's not a kindness that we can boast about, as if His kindness He works through originates in us.

Do an unmerited kindness today!!! Blow the lid off of something in kindness, or gently close the lid of a situation in kindness. It's not your kindness He's wanting to work through us . . . It's His.

1:56 A.M., wide awake.

"Papa?"

"Yeah?"

"I don't know how this is going to work..."

"It's not up to you, it's up to Me.
That's how this works... Go to sleep."

"Yes, Sir." Whew! Thanks."

"Love you..."

Daniel...really?

The Lord said for me to read Daniel 2 yesterday. So I did. I got caught up in the dream, the interpretation, possible end time ramifications, etc.

He said, "David, it's the prayer, it's Daniel's prayer for revealed knowledge so he won't be executed."

Oh. So I re-read it. It's beautiful. It's a prayer of complete trust in the Lord, not for deliverance only, but for revelation knowledge that leads to deliverance. There are times that we need heavenly knowledge to get us out of jams, even ones we don't put ourselves in. Read it.

Daniel said, "Let the name of God be blessed forever and ever, For wisdom and power belong to Him. "It is He who changes the times and the epochs; He removes kings and establishes kings; He gives wisdom to wise men And knowledge to men of understanding. "It is He who reveals the profound and hidden things; He knows what is in the darkness, And the light dwells with Him. "To You, O God of my fathers, I give thanks and praise, For You have given me wisdom and power; Even now You have made known to me what we requested of You, For You have made known to us the king's matter." (Daniel 2:20-23 NASB)

Invasion ... Gentle As It is ...

Think of an area of your life, that Jesus hasn't invaded. Doesn't matter what reason, think of an area that really screams, "Jesus, help me!!" Or maybe it's a quiet whimper of the same invocation, "Jesus, Son of David, have mercy on me!!!!! Jesus, Son of David, have mercy on me!!!!!"

And when He asks you what you need, don't hold back, open up and let the conquering King invade that area, to bring order and peace, and THEN live as more than a conqueror in Christ Jesus!!!!!

Walk boldly to the throne of Grace to receive grace and mercy in a time of need, because of extravagant favor!!!!

"David, can't sleep?"

"Nope..."

"David, don't let a person's observation turn into an accusation..."

(Couple of minutes of thoughtful silence...)

"YaaaaaaTHANKYOUPAPAwwwnnnn."

"You're welcome. Sleep now."

Gossip That Isn't Sin . . .

Today let's choose to be Gospel Gossips that talk, and talk, and talk of the greatness of God in our lives. Like on the Day of Pentecost, where we talk of the great exploits of Jesus in the Gospels, and the greatness of Him in our lives, and the impact of salvation on our lives! I want to hear the Spirit say to us at the end of the day, "Y'all are such gossips!!!"

What's Your Blood Type? OM- or J+

You know, at some point in time we are all going to be stabbed in the back. However, what type of blood flows from that wound is important. It is either the blood of the "old man" (OM-), which is anger, bitterness, hurt, rejection, fear of intimacy, and a weak scab formation trying to keep the wound opening ever present. Or, it's the Blood of Jesus (J+) that flows from us, which is grace, mercy, forgiveness, His intimacy invading the situation, and a strong healing taking place, with no adhesions of the past, tugging and pulling, trying to break the wound open.

Which blood type are you? I want to be J+!!!!

"David?"

"Yes, Papa . . ."

"Everyone has a wild stallion of money in their lives . . . majestic and scary. Most people watch it from a distance, wishful of getting close to it. Some people chase after the stallion, wildly running after it with all they have, only to end up exhausted."

"Fewer people than that, are patient enough to offer food, and rub its nose from across a gate. But once they go through the gate, the stallion bolts and darts off, because the stallion senses the people's fear of it. They fear trying to bridle it, scared of its bucking presence. So it taunts the people from a distance, "Catch me if you can, but still feed me." So they spend their life throwing food at the stallion only to be disappointed."

"And the rest of the people, the few left, have food, bridle, and gloves ready, prepared for the ride of their life. A rider bridles the stallion, and jumps on its back as fast as he can. (Others watch from a distance and are envious of these efforts.) He knows what the ride's going to be like as he takes command, and pulls on the bridle. The stallion recognizes its new master and begins to work with him. And together, almost effortlessly, they accomplish much together. Before they know it, the pasture is full of tamed stallions."

"Are you ready to ride?!"

"Yes, Sir!!!!"

What Are YOU Going to do With the Spirit Today?

But if God himself has taken up residence in your life, you can hardly be thinking more of yourself than of him. Anyone, of course, who has not welcomed this invisible but clearly present God, the Spirit of Christ, won't know what we're talking about. But for you who welcome him, in whom he dwells – even though you still experience all the limitations of sin – you yourself experience life on God's terms. It stands to reason, doesn't it, that if the alive-and-present God who raised Jesus from the dead moves into your life, he'll do the same thing in you that he did in Jesus, bringing you alive to himself? When God lives and breathes in you (and he does, as surely as he did in Jesus), you are delivered from that dead life. With his Spirit living in you, your body will be as alive as Christ's! (Romans 8:9-11 MSG)

He dwells in you in power!!!

No Comparison...

When we compare ourselves to each other, one of two things happen; we build ourselves up at the expense of tearing down another, or we tear ourselves down as we build another up. Both are idolatrous. When we compare ourselves with Jesus, it is absolutely liberating. There is no separation, division, or competition. We don't have to step up or step down to others, we step into Him. We realize that in Him we are the perfect (Bob or Suzy or James or Jennifer, etc.), and cannot be compared to any other. To do so would rob the world of who we are in Him . . . that partnership the world cannot do without. Invest all you are into the One who invested all He is into you.

Hebrews 7:25, Romans 8:27

He is Omniscient,

He knows how and when to deal with your stuff. Oh ... and everyone else's too.

So, make sure you pray that you say what you 'feel' like you need to say, so you won't regret it someday. Because what you may say was actually judgment in a way.

Don't pick on people, jump on their failures, criticize their faults — unless, of course, you want the same treatment. That critical spirit has a way of boomeranging. It's easy to see a smudge on your neighbor's face and be oblivious to the ugly sneer on your own. Do you have the nerve to say, "Let me wash your face for you," when your own face is distorted by contempt? It's this whole traveling road-show mentality all over again, playing a holier-than-thou part instead of just living your part. Wipe that ugly sneer off your own face, and you might be fit to offer a washcloth to your neighbor. (Matthew 7:1-5 MSG)

Happy Easter...really?

Jesus worked and earned His way to the cross. He obeyed all the law, all the traditions (baptism etc.), and even performed the miracles that were actually available to the Jews before His death, burial, and resurrection. (Woman bent over double, ie. daughter of Abraham, this ought not to be.) He fulfilled as many of the messianic prophecies as He could for that time. He worked my works of righteousness, so He could shed His blood and die for me. He earned for me my place into the Fathers heart by obeying Him even to the point of death. He died in my place, took my punishment, completed all that work which was required of me to have a relationship with the Father, and gave me a new life in Him. A resurrection life!

And we still say Happy Easter?!

We're so plastic...

I'm plastic, you're plastic, we're all plastic. Not like Ken and Barbie, or the Mr. and Mrs. Joe Church and family that live a fake life. We are plastic in our mind — very impressionable, but hard to impress. We treat Jesus the way we treat the world. That's what the Pharisees did — "Show us, show us a sign, perform for us . . . then we will believe." Jesus called them a wicked and perverse generation. Train a child up in the way he should go and he will not depart from it as he gets older. Children are the most plastic. Show them something in the Word infused with the Spirit and it has a lasting effect, eternal. Show them some form of pornography with an emotional event, and almost the same happens. It is deep seeded.

Why does Jesus warn us we need to have our house occupied and in order after a deliverance from a demonic stronghold? It's because we're plastic, pliable, and childlike again. Things can get seven times worse if the Spirit of God doesn't renew our mind by washing us with the water of the word, and we abide in Him as He abides in us.

As a man thinks, so is he. Out of the abundance of the heart, the mouth speaks. Don't treat Jesus like the world does . . . impress us with bigger and better. Be still and know that He is God. Allow His presence, peace, and rest to create canyons of abiding rest in your heart and mind. So when you come around your family, friends, and other people, let them be amazed at the Grand Canyon of peace, wisdom, trust and hope that God creates in you.

Are You a "Hoser" or Part of the Bucket Brigade?

Trusting in the Lord is open ended. There's no bottom to it. There isn't a finite end in trust. We trust the Lord for something to take place, but we don't stop trusting when it happens, or doesn't happen. When it doesn't, His grace has to be combined with trust. We cannot trust in and of ourselves to trust God. I see a lot of folks, including me that get tapped out pretty quickly in our own efforts. And I think that is where we sometimes fall short. We have a tendency to see ourselves as pots, urns, buckets, and the like. Even a vessel of honor is filled and emptied continuously, with a bottom in it. You know, even when we feel down . . . we scrape the bottom of our bucket. I never hear anyone say, "I'm scraping the bottom of a hose." I think I would much rather be like a pipe or a hose if I'm a vessel. Then God can point me in the direction I need to trust, where His continuous flow of grace can be ad-MINISTERED to whomever and whatever He wants. We also have to be sensitive to whether we need to mist something, or put a fire hose to a situation.

Now, in thinking back to the brigade, I believe we devised the bucket brigade in the church so we could impress God with our efforts, working hard to fill ourselves and empty ourselves, fill ourselves and empty ourselves, fill ourselves and empty ourselves. Always working, but never quite putting out all the fires. He could quite possibly want us to trust smarter and not harder, so we don't wear ourselves out, but stay rested in Him. Today, I'm going to see where He points, and how He flows through me. Imagine God having a garden hose, spraying His kids, spraying the dirt off, unforgiveness off, hurt, anger — all sprayed off. Then all joy breaks loose, "Spray me and me, me too!" And He douses us with His hose, so we can hose others! The saying, "Hey, Hoser!" now has a new meaning.

Hey, Hoser, whatcha doin' for God, eh?

He Humbles Himself ... Again!

Yesterday I looked for people to pray for, and did. I gave when He told me to give. Went to a specific church last night He told me to go to, prayed and ministered to folks. He said, "Take the pastor and his wife out to eat." Okay.

So you know what I get? God thanks me. He humbles Himself again; King of the universe, Creator of all things, King of Kings, Lord of Lords, thanks me for just obeying Him because I love Him. Things I do because I am His child, no thanks needed.

I ask, "Lord, why on Your green earth do you humble Yourself and thank me?"

His answer was, "What better person to learn humility from, than Me?"

Thanks for reading these . . .

Which way is the exit?

One of my favorite authors, Bill Johnson, says this (of course my paraphrase). "An exit sign is there to point to a greater reality, a door. We don't exit through a sign, but what it points to, a door." A sign from God leads to a greater reality, Him. The author also says, signs are there to make you wonder. Why would God want us to wonder about something in the Spirit? Isn't nature itself enough to make us wonder? Ahhh, the Grand Canyon. Isn't it beautiful? If you've ever gone down the strip in Las Vegas, those are some signs that make you wonder. That led to a greater reality . . . high electric bills, and losses at gambling that pay for the high electric bills.

John the Baptist asks Jesus if He is the One. Jesus doesn't give John a theological answer, just a list of signs that show Him being The Greater Reality.

My Dad, my heavenly Papa, is in the sign business. I want to be His apprentice. I want Him to create signs through me to make people wonder about Him. Why does God want us to wonder?

Signs that make you wonder do at least four things:

1. Shows you you're not in control.
2. Exposes your heart where you think the power source is, God or the devil or coincidence.
3. Leads to a lack of understanding, can't explain it away, it can only be God.
4. Shows us God is gooder than good.

We can be so different from Jesus. We equip the blind with everything they need but sight. He equipped them with sight so they can have everything they need. Who's really blind?
Don't treat Jesus like the world does, but treat the world like Jesus.

"Pain is Weakness Leaving the Body "

That is one if my favorite t-shirt quotes, but true only in a carnal world.

God's grace starts fresh, anew every morning — the steadfast love of the Lord never ceases, His mercies never come to an end, they are new every morning, His grace is sufficient for you, power is perfected in weakness.

Let's get real with our weaknesses to God. Just spit them out, unashamedly, unabashedly, uninhibitedly. Go boldly to the throne of Grace to receive grace and mercy in a time of need. Show the devil you're not scared of the weaknesses he has so encumbered you with. Those weaknesses will be turned and transformed into God's perfection through His power. The enemy ministers shame, rejection, and fear of being exposed to keep you locked up. Jesus broke the power of sin on the cross of Calvary, and stuffed it in the devil's face when He rose from the dead. Come into agreement with what Jesus did for you, and walk in that resurrection power. Stuff the weaknesses in the devils face!

The resurrection power of Christ causes weaknesses to leave the body!

God Isn't Scared of our Mistakes!

The mistakes that we make show that we are doing something. To practice righteousness means to work at righteousness, and know that sometimes we are going to fall short. Sometimes out of ignorance, sometimes disobedience. Proverbs 24 says, the righteous man falls seven times and still gets up. What good parent would scold a toddler for falling down when learning to walk? If you are walking down the street and trip in a pot hole and fall, do you go back to the beginning of the street and start again? Nope, you get up where you fell, dust yourself off, pick the gravel out of your hand and laugh! You can worry what people may think or say after a fall, or you can listen for the, C'mon, c'mon, come to Papa!

Do angels wear swim suits?

The angels swim and never find the shore . . .

There is a really cool worship song called "Endless Ocean" by Jonathon David Helser. In it, he sings of God's love being an ocean, an endless ocean, and a bottomless sea.

We dove over the wall in the Cayman Islands. It's like pretty sand, pretty sand, then blackness, horrible engulfing blackness. But this song describes God's love so differently. As you go deeper into the natural ocean, you get crushed to an itty bitty barely resemblance of who you were. With God's ocean of love, the deeper you go the more He expands you to the person you really are in Him. One of the last lines he sings, "You were made for this water . . ."

We really are.

Labor of love...

He worked perfectly in our place for 33 years, so He could die in our place perfectly. He was never late, or called in sick, or didn't do something because He didn't feel like it. He took on our work load, completed all our assignments, made up for all our sins and mistakes. And we still say Happy Easter?! Happy Resurrection Day!!!

Having a Bad Day?

As a believer in Christ Jesus, you are a walking, talking ark of the New Covenant of Jesus Christ. You carry the very presence of God on the inside of you. You carry the very answer to every need you and others encounter every day. You are not carried around by priests on two poles; you are carried around by Jesus Himself. You are blood covered and washed. His power emanates from you, by the Holy Spirit, so that a lost and dying generation may encounter God the same way generations encountered Him nearly 2000 years ago.
Have a GOOD day!

Yesterday Was a Tough Day!

One of the most valuable lessons I'm learning is how to live love in the moment.

Looking at the past to the Cross where the wrath of God, the wrath meant for me was poured out onto Jesus, the love of God poured out of His Son Jesus' precious blood. But that wasn't enough for God. He had to demonstrate that there was life beyond the grave, beyond Jesus becoming sin and dying in my place, in an instant. On that Sunday morning, Jesus lived love in the moment and showed us He is the resurrection and the life. Live love in the moment, there is no time like the present. He is the present and our future. Trust Him today, live love in the moment. Live the resurrection life.

"Are you rested?" He asked.

"Yes, Sir."

"Slept in, did you?" I could feel His grin.

"Yes Papa . . ."

"That is what entering My rest means, except you're supposed to do that before the answer comes. What do you feel like?"

"Peaceful, like I could lie here in this position all day long, never move, and just bask and extol Your greatness, love, mercy, kindness and provision."

"David, with Me, you rest during the battle, not afterwards. If I have already fought the battle, and you have already won, why allow the enemy to minister defeat to you? It's time to get up, but don't step out of rest, just extend it to others today."

"Thank You, Papa."

"Your eyes don't look as puffy. Amazing what My rest will do."

Death and Taxes...

There is this continuity from the Lord in our lives. We laugh at "the only thing certain in life is death and taxes." There is finality in death, but there is a continuity in taxes, estate tax, and inheritance tax that continues after we die. The continuity that I speak of is trust. God just trust us. The principle intact is; we love Him because He first loved us. We trust Him because He first trusted us.

No matter how much we screw up, He still trusts us to get it right. No matter how much we get right, He still trusts us with more. God places dreams, visions, and ideas from Him in us because He trusts us to complete them. Listen, God places dreams, visions, and ideas from Him in YOU, because He trusts YOU to complete them. Be consumed by His tsunami of trust, even if all you feel you can give back is a splash. God is waiting for you to splash Him.

He Wouldn't Even Lift a Finger to Help...

What was the force behind David's sling and that smooth stone that took down the giant? Centrifugal force and centripetal force were the natural forces. Centrifugal force being, as David swung the sling and the stone flew outward, the pouch held it in place. Centripetal force was the pull of the strap holding the pouch in place. There is a spiritual centrifugal force I'll call faith. The centripetal counterpart I can call timing or restraint, but honestly it's self doubt. It's that thing that keeps faith in the pouch and is never released . . . always swinging, every revolution a testimony to doubt's victory over me. Always saying God's gonna do something to that giant standing in front of me because of my covenant. But it's not . . . not until I lift a finger, let go of the self doubt, and trust God to hit the mark that faith is released. So instead of your days being filled with WHAT IF? . . . Lift that finger, let go, let God, and when the stone plants in the forehead of your giant, you can say, "WHAT NOW, SUCKER?!!!!!!"

And give God the credit for creating the forces of victory in the first place.
GO SLAY A GIANT!

And He Worshipped Him...

John 9 is one of my favorite chapters in the Bible. A man was born blind. Everyone but Jesus assumed it was because of his or his parent's sin. Honestly, he was born blind so sin could be committed in the womb. And yes, I know we're born with a sinful nature, but still . . . Jesus spat on the ground, made clay, anointed the man's eyes, and sent him to go wash in the pool of Siloam. But before Jesus did all that, He made the radical statement of God's true purpose, not just for this man, but everyone.

Jesus answered, "It was neither that this man sinned, nor his parents; but it was so that the works of God might be displayed in him. (John 9:3 NASB)

We are all blind to some extent. We are born blind into sin, "I once was blind but now I see." Adam and Eve were created so the works of God might be displayed in them. What is God displaying in your life today, what picture has He painted in you that will bring glory to Him?

If you read the chapter there is a big display of religious fireworks from the Pharisees. But the man born blind who now sees, keeps putting their punks out, and they can't light anymore fuses!

A most touching scene follows, where the healed meets the Healer in John 9:38, and he worshipped Him. In the temple, in front of everyone, a man worshiped what appears to be another Man. He didn't care what people thought, he worshipped Him. No music, no sound system, no "Just As I Am" in the background, nothing but the din of the temple. What worship do we display to please and glorify Him?

YOU were born . . . so that the works of God might be displayed in YOU.
Worship Him . . .

"David, I'm really not mad at you."

"I know, thank you so much."

"No, no, no I Am not angry with you not in the least little bit."

"Okay You've said that twice, I must have some hidden thought of that You're angry with me." (I feel Him smile.)

"David what part of My anger did Jesus not take on Himself, what part of My wrath did I secretly hold back, just so I could hold it just for you? What part of disappointment, hurt, frustration did I not put on Jesus? Did I not forsake Him on your account? I Am not double minded, I laid it all out on Him for you. He became your sin, so I would never be angry with you."

"Uhhh are these rhetorical questions or do I need to answer?"

"What do you need them to be?"

"None Lord, there is nothing that was not laid out on Jesus that you hold in reserve for me."

"David if you're going to talk on My ocean of love, and My bottomless sea of love, I am not going to put an Island of Anger in the middle of it. I want you to get tired swimming, so you will let go and sink and drown and die to self in My ocean of love, than trying to stay afloat on your own efforts."

"Okay so take back the water wings?"

"You're funny David."

Sniff. Sniff,

do you smell something like burning?

I was talking with Pastor Dennis of Northridge Baptist last night. He had me film one of the Bethel Boys speaking of bread, and how all the ingredients are nasty tasting individually, in and of themselves. Think of a mouthful of yeast. But when combined in a mixer, think dough hook, kneaded, left alone to rise, holes poked in you, left alone to rise again, then placed in an oven at 350 degrees for an hour . . . Sniff, sniff, you smell something? Now from that stand point life SUCKS. But what everyone one else around is seeing and hearing, is you getting made into something wonderful, filling, and appreciated.

2:06 AM

"Uhhh, God. Three clinics. Now how on earth?"

"It's not up to earth." (I feel Him GRIN)

"Papa, I'm glad you're awake now."

"If I slept I wouldn't be a very good God, somebody would miss out. And if you don't sleep you won't be a very good you. Now, shhhh. I've got the clinics, go back to sleep."

"Thank You. I'm glad you never sleep or slumber. Love you."

News Flash!!!!

We are imperfect vessels, in whom God completes His perfect will. If you think you're a failure in Him, you're probably not. If you think you don't accomplish much for God, you probably are. If you compare yourself to others you will always find a flaw, but if you compare yourself to Jesus you will always find the flawless. The world and religious people will tell you, you can't measure up to Him, He's too out of reach. That's not Jesus' invitation. I tell you the truth: you can do the same and greater. Jesus doesn't limit us to only Him . . . He un-limits us to the Father, just like He was. Paul's invitation to "be perfect as He is perfect," is the same. God wouldn't invite you to do something you couldn't complete in His grace. We have it so backwards sometimes. We try to manage Jesus, and how much He can do through us, but live our lives unchecked, undisciplined because we are told our own lives are all we can manage. You never know what God's going to do.

Accept the invitation to live holy and perfect, and do greater things. He still gets the credit. You are imperfectly perfect when He manages you!

The Three Secrets of Jesus...

Sounds mysterious, or even a bit like a tabloid headline, but it's so secret Jesus tells everyone how and what to do. In the book of Matthew, chapter 6, He lays out His three secrets of success with God, and tells it in front of God and everybody.

Don't practice your righteousness for men to see. Jesus doesn't deny a person a reward; it's either from God or man. He's simply showing us that God's reward here now, far outweighs a pat on the back from man in the here and now. Besides that, people are fickle. Remember the same people that cried, "Hosanna!" are the same ones that cried, "Crucify Him!" a week later. God's not fickle, but He is sneaky, as Bill Johnson calls Him — Jehovah Sneaky. But/and, God loves rewarding us openly what we do for Him in secret.

1. Pray secretly in your prayer closet . . . mine is my vehicle. Be careful not to tell people what you're praying about. The Father wants you to pray in secret, so you will receive your reward from Him, and not just kudos from men. And when He answers don't go brag you got what you prayed for. Take Mary's position and ponder these things in your heart.

2. Give in secret. In fact, don't let your left hand know what folded money you have in your right hand as you shake people's hands to bless them.

Don't boast about what you're giving, although some folks need to know a little about how to give secretly for discipleship purposes. But really what you give is between you and the Lord, and he rewards accordingly.

3. Fast as if you're not fasting, but feasting. Be happy, fasting curbs your appetites for self. Fasting doesn't change God's mind, it changes yours. Try an electronic fast for a few days. You will be shocked how much time you have when you're not checking texts, tweets, and FB status. Spend the time instead checking on your heavenly status. And don't tell people you're fasting. Tell them you've already eaten. Jesus' food was to do the will of the Father.

Three great secrets from the Word.

Future Piece of Ash...

You're reading this post on a future piece of ash. Whether a smart phone, tablet, computer, or book, you're looking at something that is not going to exist at some point. If you're driving and reading this, look up and around you, and pull over to finish. Look outside wherever you are, it's all going to be gone. The Bible teaches us (Paul actually), the things that you see are temporal, and the things you don't see are eternal. We get so locked up in our past, what we have seen — temporal circumstances — that it effects what we can't see, our future, which is eternal. You have a future in Jesus. I do, you do; we all do. We can't see Him, but yet He is as real as the air we breathe. And if you think you don't have the faith to look to Him and the future, your body does. That's why you just took that breath you did without consciously thinking about it. Your body breathes because it wants the future. Air is something you can't see, but yet it gives life, like Jesus. Your future is bright but not yet seen. Jesus is here, He is coming, and we will be part of a new heaven and earth. The old earth will be but ash along with our past and my iPhone. Trust Him today for your future, the eternal One.

Around and round the mulberry bush...

"Wake up a bit wound, did we?"

"Yes, Lord. I feel like "Jack" in the box. It's like I keep hearing Pop Goes the Weasel over and over but someone has their hand over the lid, Über-perseveration."

"Wow, such big words this morning! Let's keep this simple. Look "at" Me. Who's turning the crank, Me or someone else?"

"Someone else."

"Okay, now look "to" Me. Who is your peace, Me or someone else?"

"You."

"Now look "for" Me. What Am I doing?"

"You've taken that hand off the crank. You've pulled the catch back, and now You're gently pulling me out of the box intact. Wow, thanks, Lord!!!!! Who's the someone else?"

"Does it matter when you have Me?"

"Nope . . ."

Look at . . . to . . . and for Him. He loves you so, so, so greatly.

The Good News...

God knew eons ago what your problems are today and has the answer.

The bad news... The devil can keep you churned up, to slow down the manifested answer.

But the really bad news is for the devil... if Jesus lives in you, the answer lives in you, and that's really bad news for the devil.

Greater is He that lives in you, than He that lives in the world.

He Returns the Flowers...

Corrie ten Boom talks of when she gave her testimony about God's redemptive love in her life, people would come up to her afterwards and tell her what an inspiration she was ... on and on and on. She said then she would go back to the hotel room and hand each one of the compliments back to Him as if they were flowers, and when she got done He would be holding a whole bouquet of her thanks and adoration.

We cannot give anything to God without Him giving to us in the first place. We could have a room full of flowers, the compliments from others for whatever we do. We can sweep in and tell God how beautiful they are. "Here, God, the whole room is yours. Thank you. Got to go pick up the kids from soccer practice. See ya!" But the key is, Corrie took the time to give each flower of thanks individually to Him. She recognized that He took the time to give each one to her individually in the first place.

He'll turn right around and return the flowers in other ways. He loves giving to you. He loves and adores you!

Sometimes, Just Sometimes, It's Both . . .

I think a lot of our lives have been based on, "You can't have your cake and eat it too."

What did Jesus mean when he prayed, "Your will be done in earth as it is in heaven?" I think it means if it's possible in heaven, it's possible here on earth . . . that there is an answer made in heaven that fits earth problems. If there is a "well done, good and faithful servant" in heaven, can we be told that here on earth? Jesus was — at His baptism. I think God cheers us on not when we become like Jesus, but while we become like Jesus.

If it is possible to enter into the joy of my Father's rest in heaven, is it possible here on earth? If we are to lay up treasure for ourselves in heaven, can we here on earth? Accumulation of treasure isn't a wealth issue, it's a heart issue. Can we lay up treasure for ourselves on earth, as it is in heaven? I think we fear wealth, because we fear something controlling us other than God. Funny thing though, God isn't controlling, neither is He fearful of, treasure. Treasure doesn't scare God, it scares us.

We see ourselves so much differently than God. We are His treasure that channels earthly treasure where He wants it. I believe we are going to be shocked out of our gourd when we get to heaven, that there was as much available to us here in earth as in heaven that was not utilized. But because we've been taught that it's either or, we're missing out. If your heart is Kingdom minded, it doesn't matter. Be a Kingdom builder with every resource available from heaven. It's not one or the other, it's both. Fear God, not wealth. He's got deep, deep, deep pockets, and is not stingy. He's waiting on people with mustard seed size faith to do great things for Him. Oh, and you have access to it, because of Jesus, not your good works.

Figurative or Literal?

What's our take on the Gospel?
Can we live our lives in such a way that we are so available to the Spirit of God that just a glance from Him, or a whisper, can move us to lead someone to Him? To open our mouths, as Matthew 10 speaks of, and He fills our mouths with the right words to lead someone to a saving knowledge of Jesus.

The Spirit of God, who raised Christ Jesus from the dead, dwells in us. He who dwelled in Him and guided Him into all truth for 33 years, He who showed Him things to come, even His own death, burial, and resurrection, is waiting to speak through you to a lost and dying generation. He who in an instant of time hears a heartfelt prayer, an acknowledgement, and can change a person's eternal destiny, in a moment's moment. He who takes 33 perfect years, perfect death, perfect burial, perfect resurrection, and somehow infuses that life of Jesus to a person's spirit. BAM . . . they take on the nature of Christ, a new creature, all things passed away, all things new, fully righteous before God, fully accepted by God, able to live the life He does.

I don't know about you, but that makes me more attentive to Him, and less attentive to my Angry Birds score.

On Your Mark... Get Set... Wait... No, Go!!!!!!

When the wine ran out, the mother of Jesus said to Him, "They have no wine." And Jesus said to her, "Woman, what does that have to do with us? My hour has not yet come." His mother said to the servants, "Whatever He says to you, do it."
Now there were six, stone water pots set there for the Jewish custom of purification, containing twenty or thirty gallons each. Jesus said to them, "Fill the water pots with water." So they filled them up to the brim. He said to them, "Draw some out now and take it to the headwaiter." So they took it to him. When the headwaiter tasted the water which had become wine, and did not know where it came from (but the servants who had drawn the water knew), the headwaiter called the bridegroom, and said to him, "Every man serves the good wine first, and when the people have drunk freely, then he serves the poorer wine; but you have kept the good wine until now." This beginning of His signs Jesus did in Cana of Galilee, and manifested His glory, and His disciples believed in Him. (John 2:3-11 NASB)

Sometimes we're more ready than we think we are, just like Jesus. God loves working through His children unexpectedly!

Who Knew? He Does...

When God created this planet, do you think He knew just how many resources it would need to sustain us? Did you ever think that He knows that this planet could hold 20 billion people for 7 millennia? We are freaking out about resources, but He isn't. He does give us wisdom on how to be good stewards though.

He placed us in charge of this planet as stewards, not owners. God is the Owner and is in control, but we, as stewards, are in charge. He knows every mistake we are going to make, and He has provided the solution to resolve them. The solution, though, is not just knowledge, or an ageless wisdom, or even tried and true trial and error. His solution is based on relationship with Him, by Him and through Him. Yes, these solutions can come from knowledge of God, but it is more than just answers. It is rolling up the sleeves, working intimately with the Creator to accomplish something together.

Looking at the picture at the end of the ride...

"Oh, wow, Lord! Sorry for the emotional roller coaster . . ."

"I made the emotions, David, you control the ride."

"You're okay."

Jesus set aside His divinity and embraced our humanity, so we could set aside our humanity and embrace His divinity.

The scary thought is Jesus was more like you than you think, but without sin . . .
The scarier thought is we are more like Him than we think, and continue in sin . . .

Treat the world like Jesus, and not Jesus like the world . . .

Sigh...

"I'll just do whatever You want me to do."

"We've been here before, David."

"I know, and I'm still here."

"So am I. You want Me to place My hands over what you're doing. You're hands are too small to accomplish what I've put in your heart. Mine are larger and I have a bigger spread. Let me place my hands where yours are. Just rest your hands on Mine . . . just rest, and go through the motions that I'm doing. There you go— just like that."

Wait, hang on...

Oh, and don't ever back off from being a blessing. Step into it and do it.

That was random, but poignant . . .

Dropped Your Mustard Seed?

God is soooo faithful, even when we are faithless! His faithfulness makes up for our faithlessness.

You don't need an avocado pit size faith, or a coconut size faith, it's a mustard seed.

It's okay; just ask Him for another. He has a whole jar of mustard seeds in the cupboard . . .

15th Letter of the Alphabet Moment...

"Papa, you say in Deuteronomy 28 that I am to be a lender and not a borrower. How can I start lending today and not borrowing?"

"David, when you give to the poor, you lend to Me, and I repay quickly. When you or My other kids give, you meet an immediate need for someone. But it may not always be convenient for you and others who give, and I see that. So that in turn starts a return on your loan to Me. It's My Word and My principle, when you do My Word and give your principle."

"OOOOOOOOOOOOOOOOOOOOOOOOO!!"

"When you and my other kids give like that, it blesses My socks off. In fact, I'm barefoot now! I am so blessed to have so many kids who bless others. My desire is to be perpetually barefoot. Tell them to keep it up!"

The pace of peace...

There is prayer that is peaceful, and there is peace that is also paced.

Sometimes we can step into the peace of God in prayer, but that peace is paced. We feel peaceful in prayer so we step out of peace, thinking we have the peace we need to accomplish what we must.

God paces our peace to keep us on track with the pace of heaven. If we lost our peace, there are several reasons. Today think about how we may rush in and out of peace, like using peace as a pit stop. Also, we may stop, not wanting to lose the peace that is given us. But peace moves on, because it is paced by heaven.

Today stay peaceful, and stay in the pace with heaven to remain peaceful.

I Am Better Than I Am...

There is only one person we should strive to be better than, and that's ourselves. Our life in Christ today builds on who we were yesterday in Him.

This Morning I Am Praying...

"Jesus."

He answers, "David."

"Jesus."

"David."

"Jesus."

"David."

And finally I say, "What?"

He says, "I like saying your name as much as you say Mine."

Who can argue with such a Savior as He? He loves us.

What Is Faith?

Faith is merely enjoying the memories ahead of time.

One for the Road . . .

I was very sleepy driving back from Austin, Texas, to Brownwood. I didn't want to stop and nap, it was way late enough. And I didn't want to stop for an energy drink or coffee for the same reason. So I asked for the Lord's help.

Trying to keep my eyes open, I see in my mind's eye, Jesus . . . just plain as day. I see Him smile at me; I see a bust shot of him in my minds video camera. Then music started playing, a fusion, if you will, of hip hop, jazz, orchestration, last big-number- in-a-production sort of magnitude. And He starts dancing, again a fusion of the entire world's dances, moves I had never seen. Now, as if He is doing the video directing as well, the "camera" pulls back and there are four dancers in complete and perfect synchronization. Then it hits me. Heaven is about to flash mob me to keep me awake! And, now, as if on a camera boom, I'm up in the air watching tens of thousands of people all doing this dance, all copying Jesus instantaneously, fluidly. The clothing is beyond description, flowing, beautiful, and would change colors — not lights on them, but their clothing actually changed colors. It was entertaining, inspiring, joyful and full of love. Why? So I wouldn't fall asleep?

Really I have no idea. All I know is that heavenly flash mob did that for about an hour or a little more. All I could do is smile and thank Him, for a safe trip. He is truly amazing, what an incredible savior!

What's for Afters?

Acting like Jesus, and being like Jesus are two different things. Anyone can act like Jesus, adjusting their behavior to meet some religious standard. But being like Jesus comes from the inside, and the only way to be like Jesus from the inside is to get Him on the inside.

How do you invite someone in your own home? You call their name out and ask them inside. If you haven't done this, ask Jesus, out loud, to come and reside in you permanently. Believe me; He is not like your brother in law moving in. He paid for your sins a long time ago. No use hanging on to them. He's seen you do EVERYTHING, so you can't hide it from Him. And there is no shame or humiliation from Him. If you've made your home His home now, and would like some further help or direction, email me, David K. Schum at:

> davidkschumdc@yahoo.com
> subject line: IDIB book

You're loved, prayed for, paid for and have extravagant favor!!!

Additional copies are available at www.amazon.com, in both book and Kindle versions.

www.ingramcontent.com/pod-product-compliance
Lightning Source LLC
Chambersburg PA
CBHW051752040426
42446CB00007B/333